Gail Pope & Keith Hammond

Fast Food
Toys

With Values

77 Lower Valley Road, Atglen, PA 19310

DEDICATION

I would like to dedicate this book to my best friend and husband of 27 years, Frank, who endured all and who is a skilled craftsman, modeler, and collector of toys and trains, and to my sister Mrs. Linda Sue Davis, who started me on this hobby. Special Thanks to Joanne and Keith Hammond who ameliorated my collection.

Library of Congress Cataloging-in-Publication Data

Pope, Gail.
Fast food toys: with values / Gail Pope & Keith Hammond.
p. cm. -- (A Schiffer book for collectors)
ISBN 0-88740-927-X (pbk.)
1. Toys--Collectors and collecting--United States--Catalogs.
2. Premiums (Retail trade)--Collectors and collecting--United States--Catalogs.
3. Fast food restaurants--Collectibles--Catalogs.
I. Hammond, Keith, 1960-
II. Title.
III. Series.
NK9509.P66 1996
688.7'2'0973075--dc20   95-36310
CIP

Copyright © 1996 by Gail Pope & Keith Hammond

All rights reserved. No part of this work may be reproduced or used in any forms or by any means--graphic, electronic, or mechanical, including photocopying or information storage and retrieval systems--without written permission from the copyright holder.

Printed in China
ISBN: 0-88740-927-X

Published by Schiffer Publishing Ltd.
77 Lower Valley Road
Atglen, PA 19310
Please write for a free catalog.
This book may be purchased from the publisher.
Please include, $2.95 for shipping.
Try your bookstore first.

CONTENTS

Introduction 4
Using the Book 5
   Prices 6
   PVC 6
   Durability 7
   Enjoy Them! 7
How to Collect 8
   Clubs 9
Abbreviations 10
Guide to Photo Captions 10
United States Market Fast Food Toys 11
   7-Eleven 11
   Arby's 11
   Baskin Robbins 16
   Blake's Lotta Burger 16
   Bob's Big Boy 16
   Burger King 17
   Carl's Jr. 30
   Checkers 31
   Chick-Fil-A 31
   Dairy Queen 32
   Denny's 37
   Domino's 40
   Discovery Zone 40
   Dunkin Donuts 40
   Hardee's 41
   International House of Pancakes 49
   Jack-in-the-Box 50
   K-Mart 51
   Kentucky Fried Chicken 51
   Lee's Famous Chicken 51
   Little Caesar 52
   Lon John Silver's 52
   McDonald's 54
   Nathan's 86
   Pizza Hut 87
   Popeye's 87
   Roy Rogers 88
   Showbiz Pizza 90
   Sonic 92
   Subway 97
   Taco Bell 100
   Target Markets 101
   Wal-Mart 102
   Wendy's 104
   White Castle 115
Foreign Market Fast Food Toys 120
Plush and Big 129
Index 145

INTRODUCTION

In the summer of 1990 "everybody" was talking about the first set of Hardee's California Raisin figurines that had just sold for $40.00 at an auction. These things were freebies, given away in the kid's meals. They are cute. The TV advertisements were appealing, the most interesting commercial of the season. And now somebody had paid forty dollars for them.

We are a generation who have learned that anything that has ever been given away has become collectible and desirable. Toys have been given away in cereal boxes for many years. Promotions for kid's meals seem to have begun in the 1960s with activity bags and boxes and moved on to small rubber figurines, rings, and pencils, etc. These are all collectible, however indistinguishable from the same retail products. Since the mid-eighties, the fast-food chains have had well-painted and designed toys to give away, many in connection with a motion picture, TV cartoon series, or other promotion.

PVC
"ALPHA Critters® ©1987 Lloyd Gilbert Made in China"

USING THIS BOOK

EVERY TOY THAT THE RESTAURANTS OFFER IN KID'S MEALS IS HIGHLY COLLECTIBLE. Included in this book are most of the popular figurine and figurine-oriented sets that have been offered as premiums by the "fast food" and other restaurants, allowing freedom for creative expressions for the characters. The vehicles and sports interests are also included. A special section is devoted to plush and pieces which are larger than the standard 3" size. The sets show, in color, which pieces belong to which characters and which characters are in a set.

The sets are listed according to the restaurant which offered the toys in their kid's meals and/or sold them over the counter. Some of the toys were only sold by the restaurants, not used as premiums in the kid's meals. The restaurants are in alphabetical order in this book. Most of the sets are in alphabetical order according to the name of the set, but for practical or photographic reasons this is not always the case, so be sure to look around. The foreign 3" toys are in a separate section. The plush and larger-than-3" toys are in another section. The mold markings that are listed for one piece are not necessarily on all pieces in the set, there are some differences.

When there are "costumes" for the characters, they are usually two pieces that snap together around the character. Robath in the Swan Princess (Hardee's) only has one front body mask instead of the two pieces.

Some items in a set are the same figures in different colors. Only one of a color are shown for most sets with the other variations listed, unless there is a significant difference. Many of the same figurines do have slight or even major color variations due to the various dye lots of the paints used.

The size of most of these toys is about 3 inches tall or long, within an inch. Any significant discrepancy is noted in the comments with each set.

The personal trademarked characters for each restaurant are grouped together in their various sets under the restaurant's name for easy identification.

The contents of this book are the personal property of the authors who are not in any way associated with any restaurant or any reflection thereof. The restaurants are listed only as the source of the toys. This book is concerned only with the toys, not the restaurants which gave them out with kid's meals or otherwise sold them.

PRICES

It seems like the prices from many dealers are slightly down from last year as more people collect and seek out these toys. Another dealer has almost doubled his prices recently. Prices are all over the board. If you need a certain piece to complete a set or list, you might be willing to pay more for it. There are no fixed prices when you deal for collectibles — some dealers do barter. The prices listed here are some average asking prices for the toy in mint condition to MIP that dealers seem to be charging. In general the rarer-found sets, the better quality sets, the most popular characters, and the sets that have to be imported to any area seem to be worth a little more. The Under-3 toys are usually worth a lot more (2 to 5 times as much in some cases) than any in the regular offering. Usually the whole set is worth more money than the sum of the individual pieces.

PVC

There is a whole new generation of toys on the market with the invention of PVC (short for poly-vinyl-chloride, commonly used in plumbing and outdoor furniture and toys). Children's toys that are made with PVC have become practically indestructible.

PVC is slightly bendable, making toys practically unbreakable and replacing ceramic figurines on many knick-knack shelves. PVC can be molded into solid PVC figurines. Not all of the toys in this book are made from PVC; some are metal or rubber.

DURABILITY

Keeping all of these small toys in a drawer, box, or heap is no problem. I have intentionally put several of the catwoman catmobiles (McD) into the toy box with all the other toys and used a PVC rake to move them back and forth, dump them out, and toss them back and forth, etc. The thin cat's tail of the catmobile which projects out about an inch and a half has never broken off of any of these toys! Even this fragile looking projection seems to be stable and unbreakable. I am sure it would break if one intentionally applied sufficient force, but haphazard stress is withstood. The only mishaps are that some paint seems to wear off of the toys or is scrapped off by rubbing on the floor or sidewalk or a kid chews on the figurine. Another thing to watch is that some of the glued parts do separate: like the figurines on a vehicle, which can easily be repaired.

ENJOY THEM!

Display! Display! Display! With so many small toys being given away, a toy box is not sufficient. We take one shelf and display the entire set for a month. Then we put up a new series with the changing of the calendar page. After seeing Babar for a month, we switch to Matchboxes. To make things more interesting, we choose a theme — like dogs or figures on skateboards. Everybody has to hunt through their collections to contribute something. New collections are set up on another shelf or in a dollhouse/playset for all to enjoy, a new piece is added once a week, more or less, until the set is complete.

Most of the toys stay in mint condition even after being jostled. Cleaning them is a snap: if they are dirty, scrub them with an old toothbrush and scouring powder (Ajax or Comet) and water. Do NOT scrub them if the paint starts peeling! Scrubbing usually gets off all the marks while leaving the paint intact. Ink pen markings will not come off! Ink is absorbed into the plastic PVC. So please do not mark the price or names on the figurines. I thank you.

HOW TO COLLECT

To most collectors, the entire set is desirable to have. Millions, maybe even billions, of each piece are made. A lot of serious collectors only collect premiums that are left in the package — "MIP" or "mint-in-package," figuring the premium will be worth more money if left in the original wrapping. But most collectors want to be able to enjoy their collection.

If you did not get the premium at the restaurant, you can still find most of them at very reasonable prices. Prices for these premiums start as low as a dime or a quarter at yard sales, thrift stores, and flea markets. With this hobby you have to learn patience. And it takes a lot of patient hunting and searching to find them. You have to make a real effort to collect all of the sets every month from the restaurants or digging through toy boxes. There are some harder to find pieces, such as foreign toys. But many vacationers and military families bring back these toys! If you do not have time, there are many dealers who do the leg work for you and offer a good selection at toys shows, etc.

A collection like this is never complete. There are always a few undiscovered toys and more toys coming out every week.

With so many premiums on the market, start off collecting only the things you enjoy. As you find each premium, check it off in this book and make comments about it; such as the price you paid for the premium and where you found it — "bought a kid's meal on 7/20/94, on vacation in Orlando," "best friend had 2 and gave me one," "gave one to cousin Larry," "sold for 25 cents at a yard sale." Include any notes that personalize the collection for you.

Some people only go to one fast food place and collect those toys only. Some people only collect their favorite cartoon characters: only Disney, Hanna-Barbera, or Warner Brothers. Others only collect cars, Barbies, Scooby Doo, dinosaurs, jungle animals, ballerinas, angels, sports figures, sports equipment, surfing figures, flying disks, hamburger items, etc. The list and the combinations are endless and a good collection of many things has already been given away by the restaurants.

This is one hobby anyone can enjoy. Our local TV news station had one favorite toy sitting on a desk behind the newscasters. Shops, banks, secretaries, all have them sitting by cash registers or pencil boxes. Just one of these figurines can brighten up an otherwise dull view or bring a smile to a sick friend. They're not just for kids anymore. Enjoy!

CLUBS

Here are some sources that would be of some fun. When writing, include an SASE (self-addressed, stamped envelope) for information about joining the various clubs.

Angel Collectors Club of America
Pauline Neff
2689 Centennial Ct.
Alexandria, VA 22311

Burger King Kid's Club
Main Club House
P.O. Box 1527
Tucker, GA 30085-1527

Disneyana
National Fantasy Fan Club
Box 19212
Irvine, CA 92713

Drinking Glasses Collectors
Collector Glass News
P.O. Box 308
Slippery Rock, PA 16057

Club Lisa Frank
P.O. Box 5586
Tucson, AZ 85703-0586

Fisher Price Collectors Club
Jeanne Kennedy
1442 N. Ogden
Messa, AZ 85703-0586

LEGO Builders Club
P.O. Box 5000
Unionville, CT 06087-5000

Matchbox International Collectors
Association
Attention: R. Schneider
P.O. Box 28072
Waterloo, Ontario N2L 6J8 Canada
(For info, please enclose, $5)

McDonald's Collector's Club
P.O. Box 633
Joplin, MO 64802

North American Diecast Toy Collectors
Association
Dana Johnson Enterprises
POB 1824
Bend, OR 97709-1824

The Shadow Club
P.O. Box 300728
Fern Park, FL 32730

Smurf Collectors International Club
24 Cabot Rd.
W. Massapequa, NY 11758

Southern California Toy Collectors Club
1760 Termino
Long Beach, CA 90804

Star Trek Newsletter
Moonlight Design
1324 Palms Blvd.
Los Angeles, CA 90291

Toy Shop Magazine
700 E. State St.
Iola, WI 54990

ABBREVIATIONS USED IN THIS BOOK

MIP = Mint in Package — the toy comes in its plastic bag with all pieces, parts and papers.

U-3 = toys for children under the age of 3 years old.

* (before the name) = this toy is NOT pictured.

GUIDE TO PHOTO CAPTIONS

Set name and number of items per set.

Toy name with ○ to keep a checklist of items in your collection.

Restaurant which distributed the toy, year, approximate cost.

Comments, if any.

Identification marks which were cast in the mold with the toy.

7-Eleven

UNITED STATES MARKET FAST FOOD TOYS

7-Eleven & Arby's
Row 1: 7-Eleven:
○ Toy 1: Mini Disk
7-Eleven 1992, $1
Markings: "7-Eleven Slurpee® "
○ Toy 2: Triprong Flyer
7-Eleven 1992, $1
Markings: "7-Eleven (logo)"
○ Toy 3: Mr Big Bite
7-Eleven, $20-25
Mr Big Bite Holding a Slurpee.
Markings: "Mr Big Bite (logo)"
Row 1: Oscar Mayer Hot Dog Whistle-2 per set:
○ Toy 4: With Paper Band
○ Toy 5: With Molded Band
7-Eleven 1990, $2-4 each.
Markings: "Oscar Mayer (logo)"
Row 2: Babar's World Tour Finger Puppets-4 per set:
○ Toy 1: King Babar
○ Toy 2: Queen Celeste
○ Toy 3: Alexander & Zephir
○ Toy 4: Pom
Arby's 1990, $2-4 each.
All of Babar Children's books were written by the French author Laurent de Brunhoff during the 1930s and translated by Merle Haas.
Markings: "Arby's™ & ©1990 L De Brunhoff Made in China"
Row 3: Babar's World Tour Racers-3 per set:
○ Toy 1: King Babar
○ Toy 2: Cousin Arthur
○ Toy 3: Queen Celeste
Arby's 1992, $2-3 each.
About 2.25" long.
Markings: "Arby's™ & ©1992 L De Brunhoff Made in China"

Arby's

Arby's
Row 1: Babar's World Tour Squirters-3 per set:
○ Toy 1: King Babar
○ Toy 2: Alexander
○ Toy 3: Queen Celeste
Arby's 1992, $1-2 each.
Water squirters.
Markings: "™ & ©1992 L De Brunhoff Arby's® (logo) Made in China"
Row 1: Babar's World Tour Stampers-3 per set:
○ Toy 4: King Babar- "NOW READ THIS"
○ Toy 5: Zephir- "THIS BOOK BELONGS TO"
○ Toy 6: Rataxes- "MESSAGE FROM"
Arby's 1991, $3-4 each.
Rubber stampers.
Markings: "™ & ©1991 L De Brunhoff Arby's® (logo)

Made in China"
Row 2: Babar's World Tour Vehicles-3 per set:
○ Toy 1: King Babar
○ Toy 2: Zephir
○ Toy 3: Alexander
Arby's 1990, $3-4 each.
Markings: "™ & ©1990 L De Brunhoff Arby's® (logo) Made in China"
Row 3: Crazy Cruisers-Winter Wonderland-3 per set:
○ Toy 1: Yogi
○ Toy 2: Snagglepus
○ Toy 3: Cindy
Arby's 1994, $2-3 each.
Markings: "©1994 HBPI All Rights Reserved ©1994 Arby's Inc China"

Arby's

Arby's

Row 1: Little Miss-8 per set:
○ Toy 1: Little Miss Helpful
○ Toy 2: Little Miss Shy
○ Toy 3: Little Miss Splendid
○ Toy 4: Little Miss Sunshine
○ Toy 5: Little Miss Naughty
○ Toy 6: Little Miss Late
○ Toy 7: Little Miss Lucky
○ Toy 8: Little Miss Giggles
Arby's 1981, $2-4 each.
About 1.5" tall. These plush characters were also sold in stores with tapes and books.
Markings: "Arby's® (logo) ©1981 Hargraves Lic By NEA"

Row 2: Looney Tunes Car-Tunes-6 per set:
○ Toy 1: Sylvester Cat-Illac
○ Toy 2: Bugs Bunny Buggy
○ Toy 3: Tasmanian Devil Slush Musher
○ Toy 4: Road Runner Racer
○ Toy 5: Yosemite Sam Rockin' Frockin' Wagon
○ Toy 6: Daffy Duck Dragster
Arby's 1989, $2-4 each.
These are Warner Brothers characters dating back to the 1930s.
Markings: "Arby's® (logo)™ & ©WB 1989 Made in China"

Row 3: Looney Tunes Fun Figures-3 per set:
○ Toy 1: Fireman Sylvester
○ Toy 2: Freshman Daffy
○ Toy 3: Pilot Taz
Arby's 1989, $2-4 each.
Markings: "©WB 1989 Made in China Arby's® (logo)"

Row 3: Looney Tunes Holiday Figurines-3 per set:
○ Toy 4: Elf Tweety Bird
○ Toy 5: Santa Bugs
○ Toy 6: Toy Soldier Porky
Arby's 1989, $4-5 each.
Markings: "Arby's® (logo)™ & ©WB 1989 Made in China"

Arby's

Arby's
Row 1: Looney Tunes on Oval Bases-7 per set:
○ Toy 1: Pepe Lepew
○ Toy 2: Bugs Bunny
○ Toy 3: Yosemite Sam
○ Toy 4: Sylvester
○ Toy 5: Tweety Bird
○ Toy 6: Porky Pig
○ Toy 7: Tazmanian Devil
Arby's 1987, $3-4 each.
About 2" tall.
Markings: "Arby's® (logo) ©Warner Brothers Inc 1987"
Row 2: Looney Tunes Pencil Toppers-6 per set:
○ Toy 1: Sylvester
○ Toy 2: Daffy Duck
○ Toy 3: Taz
○ Also: Yosemite Sam, Porky, and Tweety
Arby's 1988, $3-5 each.
Pencil topper about 1.5" tall.
Markings: "Arby's® (logo) ©WB 1988"
Row 3: Looney Tunes Straight Legged Characters- 6 per set:
○ Toy 1: Tazmanian Devil
○ Toy 2: Elmer Fudd
○ Toy 3: Road Runner
○ Toy 4: Bugs Bunny
○ Toy 5: Daffy Duck
○ Toy 6: Willie E Coyote
Arby's 1988, $3-5 each.
Markings: "©WB 1988 Arby's® (logo)"

Arby's

Arby's
Row 1: Mr Men-10 per set
O Toy 1: Mr Bounce
O Toy 2: Mr Bump
O Toy 3: Mr Daydream
O Toy 4: Mr Funny
O Toy 5: Mr Greedy
O Toy 6: Mr Mischief
O Toy 7: Mr Nosey
O Toy 8: Mr Rush
O Toy 9: Mr Strong
O Toy 10: Mr Tickle
Arby's 1981, $2-4 each.
About 1.5 to 2" tall. Plush characters, tapes and books were sold in stores.
Markings: "Hargraves Lic by NEA ©1981 Arby's® (logo)"
Row 2: Polar Swirl Penguins-5 per set:
O Toy 1: Surfer
O Also: Snorkler, With Walkman, Wearing yellow shorts, and wearing blue shorts
Arby's 1987, $4-6 each.
Same penguin dressed in different outfits.
Markings: "Arby's® (logo) China"
Row 2: Scooby Doo Dough-3 per set:
O Toy 2: Scooby Doo
O Toy 3: Shaggy
O Toy 4: Scrappy Doo
Arby's 1994, $1 each.
TV cartoon by Hanna-Barbera.
Markings: "Made in China" Sticker: "©1994 HBPI Arby's® (logo) ©1994 Arby's Inc"
Row 3: Yogi & Friends Mini Disks-4 per set:
O Toy 1: Ranger Smith
O Toy 2: Yogi
O Toy 3: Cindy
O Also: Snagglepus
Arby's 1993, $1 each.
About 6" diameter.
Markings: "©1993 Arby's Inc ©1993 Hanna-Barbera Productions Inc All Rights Reserved:

Arby's

Arby's & Baskin Robbins & Big Boy & Blake's Lota' Burger
Row 1: Yogi & Friends Squirters-3 per set:
○ Toy 1: Yogi Bear
○ Toy 2: Cindy Bear
○ Toy 3: Boo-Boo Bear
Arby's 1994, $2-3 each.
Water squirters.
Markings: "©HBPI ©1994 Arby's Inc China"
Row 1: Pinkie the Spoon
○ Toy 4: Pinkie the Spoon
Baskin Robbins 1991, $10-15.
Markings: "Baskin 31 Robbins (logo)"
Row 2: Big Boy Sports Figures-4 per set:
○ Toy 1: Big Boy in Racing Car
○ Toy 2: Big Boy Surfing
○ Toy 3: Big Boy playing Baseball
○ Also: Big Boy Roller Skating
Big Boy Restaurants/Elias Brothers Restaurants 1990, $3-5 each.
Markings: "©1990 Elias Brothers Restaurants Inc China:
Row 2: Play Yard
○ Toy 4: Blueberry
○ Also: Strawberry, Grape, Sandbox, Slide, Swing, and Teeter-Totter
Big Boy Restaurants 1992, $4-7 each.
This was a play set with fruit "people".
Markings: "©1991 Bang a Drum Ent Mfg by Procorp Inc"
Row 3: Grimmy-6 per set:
○ Toy 1: Dog Aid
○ Toy 2: Dog Food
○ Also: "Fleas on Board (sign)" Sitting, Leash, and with Open Arms
Blake's Lota' Burger 1989, $4-10 each.
Also sold retail.
Markings: "™ & ©1989 Grimmy Inc Lic by MGM/UA 1989 DCN Ind Inc"

Burger King

Burger King
Row 1: Aladdin-5 per set:
○ Toy 1: Aladdin on the Magic Carpet
○ Toy 2: Princess Jasmine on Raja the Tiger
○ Toy 3: Jafar the Sorcerer
○ Toy 4: Genie in the Lamp
○ Toy 5: Abu the Monkey
Burger King 1992, $3-5 each.
A Disney cartoon motion picture.
Markings: "©Disney Mfg for Burger King Corp China"
Row 2: Archie Comics-4 per set:
○ Toy 1: Archie in Red Jalopie
○ Toy 2: Betty in '57 Chevy
○ Toy 3: Veronica in Corvette
○ Toy 4: Jughead in VW Bug
Burger King 1991, $3-4 each.
Comic book characters from the 1940s.
Markings: "©1991 Archie Comic Pub Inc® 1990 General Motors Corp Made in China Burger King Kid's Club (logo)"

Row 3: Barnyard Commando Cuffs-4 per set:
○ Toy 1: Major Leggar Mutton
○ Toy 2: Sergeant Short 'n' Sweet
○ Toy 3: Sergeant Woolly Pullover
○ Toy 4: Private Side o' Bacon
Burger King 1990, $2-4 each.
TV cartoons, PVC bracelets.
Markings: "Made in China™ ©TCFC Mfg for Burger King Corp"
Row 4: Beauty & the Beast-4 per set:
○ Toy 1: Beast
○ Toy 2: Belle
○ Toy 3: Chip
○ Toy 4: Cogsworth
Burger King 1992, $1-2 each.
A Disney cartoon motion picture.
Markings: "©Disney China Mfg for Burger King"

Burger King

Burger King

Row 1: Beetlejuice-6 per set:
○ Toy 1: The Uneasy Chair—BJ/Charles
○ Toy 2: The Charmer-BJ/BJ
○ Toy 3: The Ghost Host—BJ/BJ, Lydia, Delia, Charles
○ Toy 4: Peek-A-Boo-Boo—BJ/Delia
○ Toy 5: Ghost-to-Ghost TV—BJ/Jacques
○ Toy 6: Head Over Heals—BJ/Lydia
Burger King 1990, $2-3 each.
TV cartoons, two-sided to show BJ/other BJ cartoon characters.
Markings: "Made in China"

Row 2: Bone Age-4 per set:
○ Toy 1: Fangra™
○ Toy 2: T Rex™
○ Toy 3: Mastus™
○ Toy 4: Deltron™
Burger King 1988, $3-5 each.
Movable heads and tails.
Markings: "©Kenner 1989"

Row 3: Bonkers-5 per set:
○ Toy 1: Fall-Apart Rabbit
○ Toy 2: Jitters
○ Toy 3: Toots
○ Toy 4: Piquel
○ Toy 5: Bonkers
Burger King 1993, $2-3 each.
TV cartoon series, cars some in three sections each plus driver, bottoms do not mix or match different car pieces.
Markings: "Burger King Kid's Club (logo) ©Disney Mfg for Burger King Corp Made in China"

Row 4: Burger King Action Figures-4 per set:
○ Toy 1: IQ
○ Toy 2: Jaws
○ Toy 3: Kid Vid
○ Toy 4: Boomer-also came with blue skates and brown gloves
Burger King 1992, $2-4 each.
Burger King's characters.
Markings: "©1990 Burger King Corp China"

Burger King

Burger King
Row 1: Burger King All Stars Sports Kids- 5 per set:
○ Toy 1: Jaws-Football
○ Toy 2: Boomer-Ice Hockey
○ Toy 3: Kid Vid- Basketball
Row 2:
○ Toy 4: IQ-Disk Throwing
○ Toy 5: Snaps-Soccer
Burger King 1994, $1-2 each.
Three pieces each.
Markings: all pieces with "Burger King"
Row 3: Burger King Glow-in-the-Dark Trolls- 4 per set:
○ Toy 1: IQ Troll
○ Toy 2: Kid Vid Troll
○ Toy 3: Snaps Troll
○ Toy 4: Jaws Troll
Burger King 1993, $3-4 each.
Burger King characters turned into trolls!
Markings: "Burger King Kid's Club (logo) ©1993 Burger King Corp Made in China"
Row 4: Burger King It's Magic-4 per set:
○ Toy 1: Snaps' Magic Frame
○ Toy 2: Jaws Disappearing Food
○ Toy 3: IQ's Magic Trunk
○ Toy 4: Kid Vid's Disappearing Act
Burger King 1992, $1-2 each.
Markings: "Burger King Kid's Club (logo) ©1992 Burger King Corporation Made in China"

Burger King

Burger King
Row 1: Burger King Kid Transporters-6 per set:
○ Toy 1: IQ in World Bookmobile
○ Toy 2: Boomer in Super Shoe
○ Toy 3: Kid Vid in Sega Video Gamester
○ Toy 4: Wheelie in Turbo Wheelchair
Row 2:
○ Toy 5: Snaps in Camera Car
○ Toy 6: Jaws in Burger Racer
Burger King 1990, $3-5 each.
Two pieces each.

Markings: "©1990 Burger King Corp China"
Row 3: Burger King Pranks-5 per set:
○ Toy 1: Lingo's Snake-3 pieces
○ Toy 2: Jaws' Giant Spider
○ Toy 3: Boomer's Buzzer
Row 4:
○ Toy 4: IQ's Woopee Cushion-folded
○ Toy 5: Kid Vid's RC Squirter
Burger King 1994, $1-2 each.
Markings: "Burger King Kid's Club (logo) ©1993 Burger King Corporation Made in China"

Burger King

Burger King
Row 1: Burger King Top Kids-4 per set:
○ Toy 1: Kid Vid
○ Toy 2: Wheelie
○ Toy 3: Jaws
○ Toy 4: Boomer
Burger King 1993, $1-2 each.
Bottom spins off as a "top."
Markings: "©1992 Burger King Corp Made in China"
Rows 2 & 3: Burger King Water Mates-4 per set:
○ Toy 1: IQ on Dolphin
○ Toy 2: Snaps in a Glass Row Boat-2 pieces
○ Toy 3: Lingo on a Jet Ski
○ Toy 4: Kid Vid on a Raft-2 pieces

Burger King 1991, $2-3 each.
Each Kid came in two different colors as shown on the two separate shelves.
Markings: "©1990 Burger King Corp China"
Row 4: Capitol Critters-4 per set:
○ Toy 1: Muggle in Lincoln's Armchair
○ Toy 2: Jammet Jams at the White House
○ Toy 3: Max Cleans up with Jefferson
○ Toy 4: Presidential Cat Spies on the Good Guys
Burger King 1992, $2-4 each.
A short lived summer TV prime time cartoon.
Markings: "™ & ©92 SBP Made in China Burger King Kids Club (logo)"

Burger King

Burger King
Row 1: Captain Planet-4 per set:
◯ Toy 1: Captain Planet/Hoggish Greedily
◯ Toy 2: Duke Nukum/Wheeler
◯ Toy 3: Dr Blight/Mati & Linka
◯ Toy 4: Gee & Quami/Sludge-2 pieces
Burger King 1990, $2-3 each.
TV cartoons, cars flip over to reveal heroes/villains.
Markings: "©1990 TBS Prod & DIC Enter Mfg for Burger King China"
Row 2: Dino Crawlers-5 per set:
◯ Toys 1-5: No names
Burger King 1993, $1-2 each.
Wind-ups.
Markings: "Made in China Burger King Kid's Club (logo)"

Burger King
Row 1: Fast Food Miniatures-5 per set:
◯ Toy 1: Pepsi
◯ Toy 2: Fries
◯ Also: Burger King Package Fries, Hot Dog, and Whopper
Burger King 1983, $5-7 each.
About 1.75" tall.
Markings: "Russ China"
Row 1: Fun Food
◯ Toy 3: Pickle-O
Burger King, $5.
Whistle or musical instrument.
Markings: "Burger King (logo)"

Burger King

Burger King

Row 1: Gargoyles-4 per set:
○ Toy 1: Color Transformation Cup
○ Toy 2: Color Mutation "Broadway"
○ Toy 3: Spin to Life "Goliath"
○ Toy 4: Gargoyles Pop-Up book
Burger King 1995, $3-4 each.
A TV cartoon series.
Markings: "Mfg for Burger King Corp Made in China ©BVTV"

Row 2: Go-Go Gadget Gizmos-4 per set:
○ Toy 1: Copter Gadget-3 pieces
○ Toy 2: Inflated Gadget
○ Toy 3: Scuba Gadget
○ Toy 4: Surfer Gadget-3 pieces
Burger King 1991, $3-5 each.
TV cartoons.
Markings: "©1991 DIC China Mfg for Burger King®"

Row 3: Good Goblin'-3 per set:
○ Toy 1: Frankie Steen
○ Toy 2: Zelda Zoombroom
○ Toy 3: Gordy Goblin
Burger King 1989, $4-5 each.
Three pieces each.
Markings: "©1989 Burger King Corporation Made in China"

Burger King

Burger King

Row 1: Goof Troup Bowlers- 4 per set:
○ Toy 1: Goofy
○ Toy 2: Pete
○ Toy 3: PJ
○ Toy 4: Max
Burger King 1992, $2-3 each.
Disney TV cartoon series.
Markings: "Burger King Kids Club (logo) ©Disney Made in China"
Row 2: Goofy Movie-5 per set:
○ Toy 1: Goofy & Max in Water Raft-squirter
○ Toy 2: Goofy & Max on Water Skis
○ Toy 3: Goofy on Bucking Bronco
○ Toy 4: Goofy & Max in Fishing Boat
○ Toy 5: Goofy & Max in Runaway Car
Burger King 1995, $1-3 each.
A Disney cartoon motion picture.
Markings: "Burger King Kids Club (logo) ©Disney Mfg for Burger King Corp China"
Row 3: King Burger-2 per set:
○ Toy 1: King Burger Pencil Topper
○ Toy 2: King Burger Mini-disk
Burger King 1979, $5-10 each.
About 2" tall.
Markings: "©1979 Burger King Corporation"

Burger King

Burger King
Row 1: Lickety Splits Rolling Racers
○ Toy 1: Carbo Cooler
○ Toy 2: Carsan'wich
○ Toy 3: Chicken Chassis
○ Toy 4: Expresstix
○ Toy 5: Flame Broiled Buggy
○ Toy 6: Indianapolis Racer
○ Toy 7: Spry Fries
Burger King 1989, $1-2 each.
Markings: "©1989 Hallmark Cards Inc" or "©1989 Graphics Int'l Inc Made in China"
Row 2: Life Saver Freaky Fellas-4 per set:
○ Toys 1-4 No names-2 pieces each
Burger King 1991, $2-3 each.
PVC critter holds roll of Life Savers.
Markings: "©1991 Burger King Corporation Made in China"
Row 3: Lion King-7 per set:
○ Toy 1: Mufasa
○ Toy 2: Young Nala
○ Toy 3: Young Simba
○ Toy 4: Scar
○ Toy 5: Rafiki
○ Toy 6: Ed the Hyena
○ Toy 7: Pumbaa & Timon
Burger King 1994, $3-5 each.
A Disney cartoon motion picture.
Markings: "©Disney Mfg for Burger King Corp Made in China"
Row 4: Lion King Finger Puppets-6 per set:
○ Toy 1: Pumbaa
○ Toy 2: Rafiki
○ Toy 3: Simba
○ Toy 4: Ed
○ Toy 5: Mufasa
○ Toy 6: Scar
Burger King 1995, $2-4 each.
Finger puppets in pop-up boxes.
Markings: "©Disney Made in China Mfg for Burger King Corp"

Burger King

Burger King

Row 1: Little Mermaid Splash Collection-
4 per set:
○ Toy 1: Ariel on Wind-Up Sea Turtle-2 pieces
○ Toy 2: Flounder-squirter, has Burger King Kid's Club logo
○ Toy 3: Sebastian Wind-Up
○ Toy 4: Urchin Squirt Toy-squirter
Burger King 1993, $2-3 each.
A Disney cartoon motion picture & TV series. Little Mermaid was also distributed by McDonald's.
Markings: "©Disney Made in China Burger King Kid's Club (logo)"
Row 2: Matchbox Cars-4 per set:
○ Toy 1: 4x4 Mountain Man
○ Also: Ferrari (red), Ford LTD Police Car, and Corvette (yellow)
Burger King 1987, $4-5 each.
Markings: "Matchbox (logo) Mini Pick up Matchbox Toys Made in Macau"
Row 2: Mickey's Toontown Disneyland-
4 per set:
○ Toy 2: Mickey & Minnie
○ Toy 3: Goofy
○ Toy 4: Donald
○ Toy 5: Chip 'n' Dale
Burger King 1991, $2-5 each.
Wind-ups.
Markings: "©Disney Mfg for Burger King Corp China Burger King Kid's Club (logo)"
Row 3: Mini Sports Games-4 per set:
○ Toy 1: Catch mitt with Ball-4.5"
○ Toy 2: Football-4"
○ Toy 3: Basketball-1.5" diameter
○ Toy 4: Inflatable Soccer Ball-8" diameter
Burger King 1993, $1 each.
Markings: "©1993 Burger King Corp China"

Burger King

Burger King
Row 1: Nerfuls-4 per set:
○ Toy 1: Officer Bob
○ Toy 2: Bitsy Ball
○ Toy 3: Fetch
○ Toy 4: Scratch
Burger King 1989, $3-5 each.
Three pieces each: a face ball that came with a suit and a hat or hair. The Nerfuls also sold in stores with roundish houses, cars, furniture, play swings etc.
Markings: "©1985 PB Parker Brothers"
Row 2: Nightmare Before Christmas Watches-4 per set:
○ Toy 1: Christmastown
○ Toy 2: Pumpkins
○ Toy 3: Bats & Cats
○ Toy 4: Halloweentown
Burger King 1993, $4-6 each.
Watches.
Markings: "©Touchstone Pictures"

Row 3: Purr-Tenders-4 per set:
○ Toy 1: Scamp-purr on Cheese
○ Toy 2: Romp-purr, Hop-purr, & Flop-purr in Flip Car
○ Toy 3: (same car-cats flipped over)
○ Toy 4: Hop-purr on Radio-Bank
○ Also: Book
Burger King 1988, $5-7 each.
Burger King also had plush Purr-Tenders (*see Plush & Big*)
Markings: "©1988 Burger King Corp ©1987 Hallmark Cards Inc Designed by Linda Breitel/Cliff Rosenberg"
Row 4: Record Breakers-6 per set:
○ Toy 1: Accelerator
○ Toy 2: Shockwave
○ Toy 3: Fastlane
○ Toy 4: Aero
○ Toy 5: Indy
○ Toy 6: Dominator
Burger King 1990, $3-4 each.
Markings: "©1989 Hasbro All Rights Reserved 1989 Mfg for Burger King Corporation Made in China"

Burger King

Burger King
Row 1: Silverhawks-1 figurine:
○ Toy 1: Silverhawks Pencil Topper
Burger King 1987, $5-10 each.
A TV cartoon.
Markings: "©1987 Telepix"
Row 1: Simpsons-5 per set:
○ Toy 2: Homer
○ Toy 3: Marge
○ Toy 4: Bart
○ Toy 5: Lisa
○ Toy 6: Maggie
Burger King 1989, $2-3 each.
Prime Time TV cartoon series. Burger King also sold plush Simpson's characters (*see Plush & Big*).
Markings: "Made in China TM & ©1990 TCFFC"
Row 2: Spacebase Racers-4 per set:
○ Toy 1: Cosmic Copter
○ Toy 2: Moonman Rover
○ Toy 3: Starship Viking
○ Toy 4: Super Shuttle
Burger King 1989, $5-7 each.
Markings: "©1989 Burger King Corporation Made in China"

Row 3: Super Powers-1 figurine:
○ Toy 1: Aquaman
Burger King 1987, $10-15.
Markings: "©DC 1988"
Row 3: Super Powers Cup Holder-4 per set:
○ Toy 2: Darkseid
○ Also: Wonder Woman, Batman, & Superman
Burger King 1988, $10-15 each.
Figurines hold a white drinking cup.
Markings: "Darkseid is a Trademark of DC Comics Inc ©1988 Figurine Cupholder Created by Robert Demars Pat Pend"
Row 3: Teenage Mutant Ninja Turtles Bike Gear-5 per set:
○ Toy 3: Water Bottle
Row 4:
○ Toy 1: Pouch
○ Toy 2: Horn
○ Toy 3: Spike Buttons
○ Toy 4: License Plates
Burger King 1991, $2-3 each.
A TV cartoon series and a motion picture.
Markings: "Burger King Kid's Club (logo) ©Mirage Studios Made in China"

Burger King

Row 1: Pocahontas-8 per set:
○ Toy 1: John Smith
○ Toy 2: Meeko
○ Also: Pocahontas, Grandmother Willow, Governor Ratcliffe, Chief Powhatan, Flit, and Percy
Burger King 1995, $2-4 each.
Markings: "©Disney Mfg for Burger King Corp China"

Burger King

Burger King

Row 1: Teenage Mutant Ninja Turtles Rad Badges-6 per set:
○ Toy 1: Heroes in a Half Shell
○ Toy 2: Raphael
○ Toy 3: Leonardo
○ Toy 4: Donatello
Row 2:
○ Toy 5: Michaelangelo
○ Toy 6: Shredder
Burger King 1989, $4-5 each.
With suction cups.
Markings: "Mfg for Burger King Corp 1989 Excl Lic by Surge Licensing ©Mirage Studios 1989"
Row 3: Thundercats-1 figurine:
○ Toy 1: Snarf Straw Holder
Burger King 1986, $3-5.
TV cartoons.
Markings: "©1986 TPXLCI T WOLF"

Row 3: Walt Disney World-4 per set:
○ Toy 2: Mickey
○ Toy 3: Minnie
○ Toy 4: Donald Duck
○ Toy 5: Roger Rabbit
Burger King 1993, $2-3 each.
Wind-Ups, came with a parade track for the 20th anniversary for Disney World.
Markings: "©Disney Mfg for Burger King Corp China"
Row 4: Z-Bots-5 per set:
○ Toy 1: Buzzsaw
○ Toy 2: Jawbreaker
○ Toy 3: Turbine
○ Toy 4: Skyviper
○ Toy 5: Bugeye
Burger King 1994, $2-3 each.
Also came with four pogs each.
Markings: "©1993 LGTI BK China"

Carl's Jr.

Carl's Jr
Row 1: Bone A Fide Friends-4 per set:
○ Toy 1: "Steggly"
○ Toy 2: "Donney"
○ Toy 3: "Ty"
○ Toy 4: "Topsy"
Carl's Jr 1994, $3-5 each.
Dino skin "costumes" come off to reveal the skeletons, three pieces each.
Markings: "Carl's Jr® 1994 China"
Row 2: Camp California-4 per set:
○ Toy 1: Bear Squirter-squirter
○ Toy 2: Lil' Bro Disk
○ Toy 3: Mini Volleyball
○ Toy 4: Spinner

Carl's Jr 1992, $2-4 each.
Similar set distributed by Hardee's.
Markings: "Carl Karcher Ent ©92 Camp Cal China"
Row 3 & Row 4: Fun House Faces-6 per set:
○ Toy 1: Rudy Rabbit
○ Toy 2: Barney Bear
○ Toy 3: Petey Pumpkin
○ Toy 4: Glenda Ghost
○ Toy 5: Franklin
○ Toy 6: Tina Tiger
Carl's Jr 1990, $2-4 each.
You insert four fingertips into the back to move the mask
Markings: "Carl's Jr (logo) ©Carl Karchen Enterprises Inc 1990 Made in China"

Carl's Jr.

Carl's Jr & Checkers & Chick-Fil-A

Row 1: Fender Bender 500-5 per set:
○ Toy 1: Yogi & Boo Boo in Jellystone Jammer
○ Toy 2: Huckleberry Hound & Snagglepuss in Lucky Trucky
○ Toy 3: Magilla Gorilla & Wally Gator in Swamp Stomper
○ Toy 4: Quick Draw McGraw & Baba Looey in Texas Twister
○ Toy 5: Dick Dastardly & Muttley in Dirty Truckster

Carl's Jr 1990, $4-6 each.
Also distributed by Hardee's. TV cartoon series by Hanna-Barbera.
Markings: "©1990 H-B Prod Inc Lic by HPI China"

Row 2: Muppet Parade of Stars-4 per set:
○ Toy 1: Miss Piggy
○ Toy 2: Gonzo
○ Toy 3: Kermit
○ Toy 4: Fozzie

Carl's Jr 1992, $4-5 each.
Two pieces each-the characters are finger puppets which fit onto projection in car seat.
Markings: characters only: "©Henson China"

Row 3: Raging Reptiles-4 per set:
○ Toys 1-4: no names

Carl's Jr 1994, $2-4 each.
No Markings, Printed: "Carl's Jr® Made in China"

Row 3: Checkers-1 figurine:
○ Toy 5: Checkers Key Chain

Checkers Drive-In 1993, $5.
No kid's meal premiums, this key chain is sold separately and worthwhile collecting.
Markings: "China"

Row 4: African Animals-8 per set:
○ Toy 1: Monkey
○ Also: Elephant, Lion, Hippo, Water Buffalo, Ostrich, Zebra, and Giraffe

Chick-Fil-A 1991, $2-4 each.
Animal Puzzles, also distributed by McDonald's Canada.
Markings: "Chick-Fil-A® (logo)"

Row 4: Doodles Doodlers:
○ Drawing Tools-multipieces each-2 sets shown here

Chick-Fil-A 1994, $2-4 each.
Markings: "Chick-Fil-A® (logo) Chick-Fil-A Inc® 1994 Doodles® Doodlers ©Namkung Taiwan"

Row 4: Pencil Topper:
○ Toy 3: Chick-Fil-A Pencil Topper

Chick-Fil-A 1992, $2-4.
Markings: "Chick-Fil-A Inc® 1992 ©Namkung 1992 Taiwan"

Chick-Fil-A

Chick-Fil-A & Dairy Queen
Row 1: Dino Puzzles-6 per set:
○ Toy 1: Bronto
○ Toy 2: Stego
○ Also: 4 others
Chick-Fil-A 1993, $2-4 each.
Puzzles.
Markings: "Chick-Fil-A® (logo)"
Row 1: A Farm Puzzle-7 per set:
○ Toy 3: Goat
○ Also: Cow, Horse, Pig, Sheep, Farmer, and Tractor
Chick-Fil-A 1992, $2-4 each.
Puzzles.
Markings: "Chick-Fil-A® (logo)"
Row 2: Richard Scarry Molds-5 per set:
○ Toy 1: Lowly Worm™
○ Toy 2: Mr Fumble™
○ Toy 3: Heckle Cat™
○ Toy 4: Sergeant Murphy™
○ Also: Hilda Hippo™

Chick-Fil-A 1993, $2-4 each.
Playdough or sand molds.
Markings: "©1993 R Scarry Chick-Fil-A®"
Row 3: Balance Buddies:
○ Toy 1-5: 1set of Balance Buddies-5 pieces
Dairy Queen 1994, $1-2.
Stacking Circus figures, also distributed by McDonald's.
No Markings
Row 4: Bear Water Color Set:
○ Toy 1: Bear Water Color Set
Dairy Queen 1993, $1-3.
About 5" tall, water colors are on a palette in the bear case.
Markings: "Made in China"
Row 4: Bloom Ball:
○ Toy 2: Bloom Ball
Dairy Queen 1994, $1-2.
About 2.5" diameter.
No Markings

Dairy Queen

Dairy Queen
Row 1: Circus Train
○ Toy 1: Engine
○ Toy 2: Car/Cage
○ Toy 3: Car/Cage
○ Toy 4: Caboose
Dairy Queen 1994, $4-5 each.
Peel-off stickers for each window, pieces attach together.
Markings: "Made in China"
Row 2: Creative Child Cards-4 per set:
○ Toy 1: ABC Flash Cards
○ Toy 2: Crazy Eights
○ Toy 3: Fish
○ Toy 4: Old Maid
Dairy Queen 1993, $1-2 each.
Playing Cards, also distributed by Hardee's.
Row 3: Dairy Queen Toys-4 per set:
○ Toy 1: Dinosaur Bubbler
○ Toy 2: Yo-Yo
○ Also: Spinner & Book
Dairy Queen 1994, $1-2 each.
Different dinosaurs on the bubbler.
Markings: " ©1992 Dorda Ind Ltd Made in China"
Row 3: Dennis Deck:
○ Toy 3: Dennis Deck Playing Cards
Dairy Queen 1994, $3-4.
Printed: "® Am DQ Corp ©Am DQ Corp Hank Ketcham Enterprises Inc"
Row 4: Dennis The Menace-4 per set:
○ Toy 1: Dennis in Fire Truck
○ Toy 2: Margaret in Astronaut's suit-3 pieces
○ Toy 3: Ruff in Dino costume-3 pieces
○ Toy 4: Joey in #7 Race Car
Dairy Queen 1994, $3-5 each.
Markings: "©Katcham Made in China"

Dairy Queen

Dairy Queen

Row 1: Dennis The Menace Christmas Ornaments
- Toy 1: Dennis with Joey in Stocking
- Toy 2: Dennis with Candy Cane
- Toy 3: Dennis with Wreath
- Toy 4: Dennis Wrapping Gifts

Dairy Queen 1994, $2-4 each.
Markings: "® Ketcham"

Row 2: Dinosaur Trolls:
- Toys 1-5: No names-Boys & Girls

Dairy Queen 1993, $2-4 each.
Boy and Girl Dinos with four different colors of hair "Collect them all."
Markings: "China"

Row 3: Dogs:
- Toy 1: German Shepherd
- Toy 2: Dalmatian
- Also: Others

Dairy Queen 1995, $1-2 each.
Markings: dog name and "China"

Row 3: DQ Spinners-4 per set:
- Toy 3: Strawberry Bear
- Also: Butterscotch Beaver, Chocolate Chimp, and Marshmallow Moose

Dairy Queen 1992, $1-2 each.
Markings: "©CDM 1992 China"

Row 3: Funbunch-2 per set:
- Toy 4: Single Ice Cream Cone Whistle
- Toy 5: Double Ice Cream Cone Whistle

Dairy Queen 1991, $2-3 each.
Markings: "Dairy Queen DQ Canada"

Row 4: The Jetsons-4 per set:
- Toy 1: Elroy's™ Intergalactic Twirler
- Toy 2: Rolling Rosie™
- Toy 3: Astro's™ Treadmill Workout
- Toy 4: George & Jane's™ Space Sphere

Dairy Queen 1995, $3-5 each.
Inflatable Space Sphere is about 7" in diameter-shown deflated.
Markings: "The Jetsons™ (logo) ©1995 HBPI China"

Dairy Queen

Dairy Queen
Row 1: Kid's Pick-nic!-4 per set:
Toy 1: Puppy in My Pocket™-2 pieces
Toy 2: GI Joe™
Toy 3: Transformers® Robots in Disguise
Toy 4: Kitty Surprise® -2 pieces
Dairy Queen 1995, $2-4 each.
Markings: "Puppy in My Pocket™ ©1994 Morrison Entertainment Group Inc"
Row 2: Mix and Match Dinosaurs-4 per set:
Toy 1: Brontosaurus
Toy 2: Pteradactyl
Toy 3: Tyranosaurus Rex
Toy 4: Stegosaurus
Dairy Queen 1993, $2-4 each.
Also given out by White Castle and Carl's Jr.
No Markings
Row 3: Number Transformers-10 per set:
Toy 1: Number 3
Also: all numbers from 1 to 10
Dairy Queen 1993, $2-4 each.
Number blocks transform into robots.
No Markings
Row 3: Pullback Racers-6 per set:
○ Toy 2: Bee
○ Toy 3: 3 Stacked Doves
○ Toy 4: Tire with Wings
○ Toy 5: Chevy logo with 4 Stars
○ Toy 6: Flame
○ Also: one other
Dairy Queen 1993, $2-4 each.
2" long each in various colors with different decals on hood of racer.
Markings: "Made in China"
Decal: "Dairy Queen"
Row 4: Radio Flyer
○ Toy 1: Radio Flyer Wagon
Dairy Queen 1991, $3-5 each.
About 4" long plus handle.
No Markings.
Decals: "Dairy Queen" and "Radio Flyer"

Dairy Queen

Dairy Queen
Row 1: Rock-A-Doodle-6 per set:
○ Toy 1: Chanticleer
○ Toy 2: Patou
○ Toy 3: Edmund
○ Toy 4: Peepers
○ Toy 5: The Grand Duke of Owl
○ Toy 6: Sniper
Dairy Queen 1992, $5-8 each.
A human-and-cartoon motion picture.
Markings: "™ ©1992 Goldcrest Animation Ltd Made in China"
Row 2: Space Shuttle-4 per set:
○ Toys 1-4: Space Shuttle

Dairy Queen 1993, $2-4 each.
Same model in different colors with different decals.
Markings: "ST® (logo) Copyright Pat Pending Made in China"
Row 3: Tom & Jerry-6 per set:
○ Toy 1 Tom-squirter
○ Toy 2: Tom-stamper
○ Toy 3: Tom in Sports Car
○ Toy 4: Jerry in Sports Car
○ Toy 5: Jerry-stamper
○ Toy 6: Jerry-squirter
Dairy Queen 1993, $2-5 each.
Markings: "©1993 TEC Made in China"

Denny's

Denny's

Row 1: Denny's Stencils
- Toy 1: The Jetsons
- Toy 2: Sealife

Denny's, $1-2 each.
Markings: "Denny's® (logo)"

Row 2: Flintstones Dino-Makers–6 per set:
- Toy 1: Tyranosaurus Rex
- Toy 2: Triceratops
- Toy 3: Pteradactyl
- Toy 4: Stegosaurus
- Toy 5: Brontosaurus
- Toy 6: Mastodon

Denny's 1991, $3-4 each.
Two or three parts pop together to let sections turn or twist.
Markings: "Denny's® ©1991 H-B Prod Inc Lic by HPI Made in China"

Row 3: Flintstones Dino-Racers–6 per set:
- Toy 1: Pebbles
- Toy 2: Fred
- Toy 3: Dino
- Toy 4: Betty
- Toy 5: Barney
- Toy 6: Bamm-Bamm

Denny's 1991, $3-5 each.
Markings: "Denny's® ©1991 H-B Prod Inc Lic by HPI Made in China"

Row 4: Flintstones Fun Squirters–6 per set:
- Toy 1: Fred
- Toy 2: Wilma
- Toy 3: Bamm-Bamm
- Toy 4: Dino
- Toy 5: Barney
- Toy 6: Pebbles

Denny's 1991, $2-3 each.
Squirters.
Markings: "Denny's® ©1991 H-B Prod Inc Lic by HPI Made in China"

Denny's

Denny's
Row 1: Flintstones Rock & Rollers-6 per set:
○ Toy 1: Fred
○ Toy 2: Dino
○ Toy 3: Bamm-Bamm
○ Toy 4: Mastodon
○ Toy 5: Barney
○ Toy 6: Pebbles
Denny's 1991, $3-5 each.
Markings: "©1991 H-B Prod Inc Denny's® China Lic by HPI"
Row 2: Flintstones Glacier Gliders-6 per set:
○ Toy 1: Pebbles
○ Toy 2: Barney
○ Toy 3: Fred
○ Toy 4: Bamm-Bamm
○ Toy 5: Hoppy
○ Toy 6: Dino
Denny's 1990, $3-5 each.
Markings: "©1990 Hanna-Barbera Prod Inc Lic by Hamilton Projects Inc Mfg by Irvine Ca Made in China"
Row 3: Flintstone Stone Age Cruisers-6 per set:
○ Toy 1: Fred
○ Toy 2: Barney
○ Toy 3: Bamm-Bamm
○ Toy 4: Dino
○ Toy 5: Wilma
○ Toy 6: Pebbles
Denny's 1991, $3-5 each.
Markings: "Denny's® ©1991 H-B Prod Inc Lic by HPI China"
Row 4: Flintstones Vehicles-6 per set:
○ Toy 1: Fred
○ Toy 2: Barney
○ Toy 3: Dino
○ Toy 4: Bamm-Bamm
○ Toy 5: Pebbles
○ Toy 6: Wilma
Denny's 1990, $3-5 each.
Markings: "©1990 H-B Prod Inc Lic by HPI China"

Denny's

Denny's
Row 1: Jetson Planet Balls-6 per set:
○ Toy 1: Jupiter-Judy
○ Toy 2: Saturn-George
○ Also: Earth-Jane, Moon-Astro, Mars-Elroy, and Neptune-Rosie
Denny's 1992, $2-4 each.
One character is printed on each planet ball with some planet info.
No Markings, Printed: "Denny's® (logo)"
Row 2: Jetson Puzzle Ornaments-6 per set:
○ Toy 1: Astro
○ Toy 2: Elroy
○ Toy 3: Judy
○ Toy 4: Rosie
○ Toy 5: George
○ Toy 6: Jane
Denny's 1992, $3-4 each.
Each came in green and purple. K-Mart also distributed similar puzzles.
Markings: "©1992 Denny's Inc® & ©1992 H-B Prod Inc China"
Row 3: Jetson's Spacecards-6 per set:
○ Toy 1: Constellations (cards)
○ Toy 2: Astronomers (cards)
○ Toy 3: Mission Crews (case)
○ Also: Spacecraft, Planets, and Phenomenon
Denny's 1992, $1-3 each.
Each came with several round cards and a round case.
Markings: "©1992 Denny's Inc® & ©H-B Prod Inc Made in China"
Row 4: Spinner:
○ Toy 1: Denny's Spinner
Denny's 1993, $2-4 each.
Markings: "Denny's® (logo) ©1993 Denny's Inc Made in China"

Domino's

Domino's & Discovery Zone & Dunkin' Donuts
Row 1: Noids
○ Toy 1: Noid Book Mark
○ Toy 2: 4" Bendable Noid
○ Toy 3: Noid Mini Disk
○ Toy 4: 6" Window Noid
Domino's Pizza 1986-1993, $3-5 each.
Markings: "©1986 Domino's Pizza All Rights Reserved"
Row 2: Noid PVCs-7 per set:
○ Toy 1: Sorcerer Noid
○ Toy 2: Jack-Hammer Noid
○ Toy 3: Mad Bomber Noid
○ Toy 4: Angry Noid on Domino's Pizza Box-2 pieces
○ Toy 5: Annoyed Noid
○ Toy 6: Boxer Noid
○ Toy 7: Ear-Pulling Noid
Domino's Pizza 1987, $3-5 each.
Markings: "©1987 Domino's Pizza All Rights Reserved"
Row 3: Discovery Zone:
○ Toy 1: Spinner
○ Toy 2: Dan Marino Football Player
○ Toy 3: Hackeysack Ball
Discovery Zone 1994, $1-3 each.
Hackeysack balls also distributed by Showbiz and Subway.
Markings: "Discovery Zone® (logo)"
Row 4: Munchkins-4 per set:
○ Toy 1: Beach Munchkin
○ Toy 2: Skateboard Munchkin
○ Toy 3: Baseball Munchkin
○ Also: Lady Munchkin
Dunkin' Donuts 1989, $6-10 each.
Markings: "Dunkin' Donuts Inc Made in China ©1989 Martex Corp All Rights Reserved"

Hardee's

Hardee's
Row 1: Beach Bunnies-4 per set:
O Toys 1-4 No names
Hardee's 1989, $2-4 each.
Markings: "Beach Bunnies™ ©1989 Applause Inc China"
Row 2: Beakman's World-4 per set:
O Toy 1: It's a Magnetic World!-3 pieces-inside: horseshoe magnet
O Toy 2: D'Facts of Light!-3 pieces-inside: prism with Lester the Ratman's head on top
O Toy 3: Beakman's Whirl!
O Also: Physics Follies!
Hardee's 1995, $2-4 each.
No Markings
Row 3: California Raisins I-4 per set:
O Toy 1: Lead Singer with Mike
O Toy 2: Conga Dancer with Blue Shoes
O Toy 3: Sax Player
O Toy 4: Conga Dancer with Orange Glasses
Hardee's 1987, $1-12 each.
A set of these MIP sold for $40 at auction in 1990, placing kid's meal premiums into prominence.
Markings: "©1987 CALRAB Mfg Applause Inc China"
Row 4: California Raisins
O Toy 1: Lead Singer with Mike
O Toy 2: Conga Dancer with Orange Glasses
O Toy 3: Sax Player
O Toy 4: Conga Dancer with Blue Shoes
Post Raisin Brand 1987, $1-8 each.
These are included to show the size difference. The characters are the same, Hardee's Raisins are more petite.
Markings: "©1987 CALRAB Mfg Applause Inc China"

Hardee's

Hardee's
Row 1: California Raisins II-6 per set:
○ Toy 1: Trumpy Trunote
○ Toy 2: Captain Toonz
○ Toy 3: FF Strings
○ Toy 4: Waves Weaver
○ Toy 5: SB Stuntz
○ Toy 6: Rollin' Rollo
Hardee's 1988, $3-5 each.
Second California Raisin offering.
Markings: "©1988 CALRAB Mfg Applause Inc China"
Row 2: California Raisins IV-4 per set:
○ Toy 1: Buster
○ Toy 2: Alotta Stile
○ Toy 3: Anita Break
○ Toy 4: Benny
Hardee's 1991, $3-5 each.
Raisins III is in the Plush & Big section.

Markings: "The Ca Raisins™ ©CALRAB Lic/Mfg by Applause China"
Row 3: Camp California-4 per set:
○ Toy 1: Mini Disk
○ Toy 2: Bear-squirter
○ Toy 3: Mini Volleyball
○ Toy 4: Spinner
Hardee's 1993, $2-3 each.
This set is similar to the Camp California set distributed by Carl's Jr.
Markings: "©1992 Camp Cal China"
Row 4: Days of Thunder-4 per set:
○ Toy 1: City Chevy #46
○ Toy 2: Hardee's #18
○ Toy 3: Mello Yello #51
○ Toy 4: Superflo #46
Hardee's 1990, $4-6 each.
Markings: "Matchbox® (logo) Matchbox Int'l Ltd ©1990"

Hardee's

Hardee's
Row 1: Dinos
○ Toy 1: Bronto
○ Toy 2: Steggy
○ Also: Rex and Tops
Hardee's 1994, $1-2 each.
Movable with three pieces each.
Markings: "©1994 HFS"
Row 1: Dinosaur in My Pocket-4 per set:
○ Toy 3: Stegosaurus
○ Toy 4: Triceratops
○ Toy 5: Brontosaurus
○ Toy 6: Tyrannosaurus Rex
Hardee's 1993, $1-2 each.
About 2".
Markings: "93 MEG 93 HFS China"
Row 2: Eek! The Cat-3 per set:
○ Toy 1: Eek! The Cat-arms move
○ Toy 2: Annabelle
○ Toy 3: Sharky-squirter
Hardee's 1995, $2-4 each.
Distributed at the same time with The Terrible Thunderlizards, A TV cartoon series.
Markings: "™ & ©FCN Inc 1995 Hardee's Dakin/China"

Row 3: Eureeka's Castle Stampers-4 per set:
○ Toy 1: Magellan-"Heart" stamp
○ Toy 2: Eureeka-"Star" stamp
○ Toy 3: The Moat Twins-"Circle" stamp
○ Toy 4: Batly-"Square" stamp
Hardee's 1994, $2-4 each.
Stampers.
Markings: "Eureeka's Castle™ on Nick Jr® Made in China Mfg by Dakin ©1994 Nickelodeon"
Row 4: Fender Bender 500-5 per set:
○ Toy 1: Yogi & Boo Boo in Jellystone Jammer
○ Toy 2: Huckleberry Hound & Snagglepuss in Lucky Trucky
○ Toy 3: Magilla Gorilla & Wally Gator in Swamp Stomper
○ Toy 4: Dick Dastardly & Muttley in Dirty Truckster
○ Toy 5: Quick Draw McGraw & Baba Looey in Texas Twister
Hardee's 1990, $4-6 each.
TV cartoon series by Hanna-Barbera, also distributed by Carl's Jr.
Markings: "©1990 H-B Prod Inc Lic by HPI China"

Hardee's

Hardee's

Row 1: Flintstones First Thirty Years-5 per set:
- Toy 1: Fred & TV
- Toy 2: Pebbles & Telephone
- Toy 3: Barney & Barbecue
- Toy 4: Bamm-Bamm & Pinball Machine
- Toy 5: Dino & Jukebox

Hardee's 1991, $3-5 each.
TV cartoon series by Hanna-Barbera, two pieces each, about 2" tall.
Markings: "©1991 H-B Prod Inc China"

Row 2: Food Squirters 90-4 per set:
- Toy 1: Hamburger
- Toy 2: Fries
- Toy 3: Strawberry Shake
- Toy 4: Hot Dog

Hardee's 1990, $1-3 each. Toy #4, $4-5.
Water squirters. The hot dog had limited distribution.
Markings: "Hardee's ©1990 Made in China"

Row 2: Food Squirters 93-4 per set:
- Toy 5: Hamburger
- Toy 6: Fries
- Toy 7: Shake
- Also: Hot Dog

Hardee's 1993, $2-3 each. Hot Dog, $4-5.
Fluorescent, same mold as originals. The hot dog had limited distribution.
Markings: "©1990 Made in China Hardee's"

Row 3: Ghostbusters II-4 per set:
- Toy 1: Ghostbuster Siren
- Toy 2: Ghostbuster Siren
- Also: in red and white

Hardee's 1989, $2-4 each.
Recalled. Each has a different electronic sound.
Markings: "Made in Taiwan"

Row 3: Kazoo Crew Sailors-4 per set:
- Toy 3: Captain
- Toy 4: Crewman
- Toy 5: Look-Out
- Toy 6: First Mate

Hardee's 1991, $3-5 each.
Whistles about 5" tall. All have an "H" on them.
Markings: "Lic & Mfg by Applause China"

Hardee's

Hardee's
Row 1: Marvel Comics-4 per set:
○ Toy 1: She-Hulk
○ Toy 2: Mr America
○ Toy 3: Spiderman
○ Toy 4: Hulk
Hardee's 1992, $3-5 each.
Comic book characters. All came with and without the decals on the vehicles.
Markings: "©1990 Marvel Irvine Ca Made in China"
Row 2: Micro Super Soaker-4 per set:
○ Toy 1: Water Cannon
○ Toy 2: Water Gun
○ Toy 3: Bow & Arrow
○ Toy 4: Soak 'n' Fly
Hardee's 1994, $1-2 each.
Squirters.
Markings: "©1994 Larami Corp Lic by LCI Inc ©1994 Hardee's Food Systems Inc Made in China"
Row 3: Muppets Christmas Carol-4 per set:
○ Toy 1: Miss Piggy-as Mrs Kratchet
○ Toy 2: Kermit-as Tiny Tim
○ Toy 3: Gonzo-as Eboneezer Scrooge
○ Toy 4: Fozzie-as Bob Kratchet
Hardee's 1993, $1-2 each.
Finger puppets.
Markings: "©Henson Dakin Made in China"
Row 3: Nicktoons Cruisers-8 per set:
○ Toy 5: Spunky™
○ Toy 6: Tommy Pickles™
Row 4:
○ Toy 1: Ren Hoek™
○ Toy 2: Stimpy™
○ Toy 3: Angelica Pickles™
○ Toy 4: Porkchop™
○ Toy 5: Doug Funnie™
○ Toy 6: Rocko™
Hardee's 1994, $3-5 each.
TV cartoons.
Markings: "©1994 Nickelodeon 1994 Hardee's Dakin/China"

Hardee's

Row 1: Nicktoons Bookmarks-4 per set:
○ Toy 1: Rocko™ & Spunky™
○ Also: Ren & Stimpy, Porkchop & Doug, and Tommy and Angelica

Hardee's 1994, $3-5 each.
Markings: "©1994 Nickelodeon 1994 Hardee's Dakin Mfg by Dakin Inc"

Row 1: Road Runner
○ Toy 2: Road Runner

Hardee's 1993, $4
Markings: "The Ertle Co® Dyersville Iowa USA Made in Taiwan Chevrolet Camero Replica"

Row 1: Smurfs
○ Toys 3-6
Row 2: Smurfs
○ Toys 1-8
Row 3: Smurfs
○ Toys 1-6

Hardee's 1990, $3-5 each.
This is just a sampling of the Smurfs available. Over 100 different Smurfs were given out in Hardee's kid's meals! No list is available. Smurfs were created by Schleich in Germany and very popular in Europe. Hanna-Barbera made them into the TV cartoon series. All Smurfs are made by Peyo and all are highly collectable. *Markings:* "©Peyo"

Row 3: Christmas Elves:
○ Toys 7 & 8: Christmas Elves

Retail 1978, $3-5 each. These are NOT early Smurfs. Compare the size of their eyes and noses. Christmas Elves are made by Empire and are worthwhile collecting by themselves!
Markings: "(Empire Crown-logo)® Empire ©1978 (Heart-logo) Made in Hong Kong"

Row 4: Smurfs on Skateboards-6 per set:
○ Toy 1: Papa Smurf
○ Toy 2: Swimming Smurf
○ Toy 3: Surfing Smurfette
○ Toy 4: Standing Tall Smurf
○ Toy 5: Bikini Smurfette
○ Toy 6: Puppy

Hardee's 1990, $3-5 each. Smurfs are named by their activity, these came with a peel-off sticker: "Smurf®"
Markings: "Smurf® ©Peyo Licensed by Applause Licensing China"

Hardee's

ardee's
ow 1: Snowballs-4 per set:
○ Toy 1: Stove Pipe Hat
○ Toy 2: Ski Cap & Goggles
○ Toy 3: Yankee Cap with Ear Flaps
○ Toy 4: Scottish Tam
ardee's 1994, $2-3 each.
Water squirters, white but change color when wet or cold.
Markings: "Use Ice Water ©1994 Hardee's Food Systems Inc"

ow 2: Speed Bunnies-4 per set:
○ Toy 1: Cruiser-Roller Blades
○ Toy 2: Dusty-Skateboard
○ Toy 3: Sunny-Wind Surfer
○ Toy 4: Stretch-Speed Walker
ardee's 1994, $1-2 each.
Markings: "©1993 HFS China"

ow 3: Swan Princess-5 per set:
○ Toy 1: Prince Derek
○ Toys 2 & 3: Princess Odette/Swan-skirt flips over (both views shown)
○ Toy 4: Jean-Bob-2 pieces
○ Toy 5: Puffin-walker
○ Toy 6: Rothbart-2 pieces: Rothbart & body mask
Hardee's 1994, $2-3 each.
A cartoon motion picture.
Markings: "©1994 Nest Inc Lic by LCI Inc ©1994 Hardee's Food Systems Inc Made in China"

Row 4: Tang Mouth-4 per set:
○ Toy 1: Lance
○ Toy 2: Tag
○ Toy 3: Flap
○ Toy 4: Awesome Annie
Hardee's 1991, $3-5 each.
Markings: "Tang™ ©General Foods Mfg Applause Inc China"

Hardee's

Hardee's

Row 1: Tattoads-4 per set:
○ Toy 1: Toadette
○ Toy 2: Toadinator
○ Toy 3: Toad-Dude
○ Toy 4: Toadster

Hardee's 1995, $1-2 each.
Each came with tattoo stickers for toads or kids.
Markings: "©1994 Hardee's Food Systems Inc Made in China"

Row 2: The Terrible Thunderlizards-3 per set:
○ Toy 1: Squatt
○ Toy 2: Kutter
○ Toy 3: Doc
○ Toy 4: Launcher-1 came with each Thunderlizard

Hardee's 1995, $1-3 each.
Launchers. This set was distributed simultaneously with Eek! The Cat, TV cartoon series.
Markings: "™ & ©1995 FCN Inc 1995 Hardee's Dakin/China"

Row 3: Treasure Trolls-6 per set:
○ Toys 1-6: No names

Hardee's 1993, $1 each. Six different hair colors and four different symbols on their tummies: star, heart, circle, and diamond. Also distributed by Long John Silvers, Roy Rogers, Sonic, and Wal-Mart.
Markings: "China"

Row 4: Where's Waldo-4 per set:
○ Toy 1: Waldo
○ Toy 2: Wenda
○ Toy 3: Wizard
○ Toy 4: Woof

Hardee's 1991, $3-5 each. Straw sliders.
Markings: "©MH 91 China"

Hardee's

Row 1: X-Men-4 per set:
○ Toy 1: Cyclops vs Commando
○ Toy 2: The Blob vs Wolverine
Row 2:
○ Toy 3: Phantasia vs Storm
○ Toy 4: Rogue vs Avalanche
Hardee's 1995, $3-5 each.
Three pieces each. Also distributed by Roy Rogers.
Markings: "™ & ©1995 Marvel 1995 Hardee's Dakin/China"

Hardee's

International House of Pancakes

Row 1: Pancake Kids-10 per set:
○ Toy 1: Cynthia Cinnamon Apple
○ Toy 2: Chocolate Chip Charlie
○ Toy 3: Susie Strawberry
○ Toy 4: Bonnie Blueberry
○ Toy 5: Harvey Harvest
Row 2:
○ Toy 6: Betty Buttermilk
○ Toy 7: Frenchy
○ Toy 8: Rosanna Bananna Nut
○ Toy 9: Peter Potato
○ Toy 10: Von der Gus
International House of Pancakes 1992, $3-5 each.
Markings: "IHOP® Restaurant Made in China"

Row 3: Pancake Kid Cruisers-8 per set:
○ Toy 1: Chocolate Chip Charlie
○ Toy 2: Betty Buttermilk
○ Toy 3: Harvey Harvest
○ Toy 4: Susie Strawberry
Row 4:
○ Toy 5: Bonnie Blueberry
○ Toy 6: Frenchy
○ Toy 7: Von der Gus
○ Toy 8: Cynthia Cinnamon Apple
International House of Pancakes 1994, $3-5 each.
There was also a set of three plush Pancake Kids (not shown).
Markings: "©1993 International House of Pancakes Made in China"

Jack-in-the-Box

Jack-in-the-Box
Row 1: Jack Pack Bendable Buddies 91-
5 per set:
○ Toy 1: Jumbo Jack
○ Toy 2: Sly Fry
○ Toy 3: Ollie O Ring
○ Toy 4: Edgar E Eggroll
○ Toy 5: Betty Burger
Jack-in-the-Box 1991, $5-15 each.
Markings: "Jack-in-the-Box® (logo) Made in China"
Row 2: Jack Pack Bendable Buddies 92-
5 per set:
○ Toy 1: Sly Fry
○ Also: Jumbo Jack, Ollie O Ring, Betty Burger, and Edgar E Eggroll
Jack-in-the-Box 1992, $5-15 each.
Markings: "Jack-in-the-Box® (logo) Made in China"
Row 3: Jack-in-the-Box People-5 per set:
○ Toy 1: Jack
○ Toy 2: Spy
○ Toy 3: Clown
○ Toy 4: German
○ Toy 5: O Ring
Jack-in-the-Box 1980s, $13-20 each.
Bendables. Note: these were all found on the east coast-they travell
Markings: "Jack-in-the-Box® Imperial (Crown-logo) Hong Kong"
Row 4: Jack Pack Finger Puppets-5 per set:
○ Toy 1: Jumbo Jack
○ Toy 2: Sly Fry
○ Toy 3: Ollie O Ring
○ Toy 4: Edgar E Eggroll
○ Toy 5: Betty Burger
Jack-in-the-Box 1993, $5-10 each.
Finger puppets.
Markings: "Jack-in-the-Box® (logo) Made in China"

K-Mart

K-Mart & Kentucky Fried Chicken & Lee's Famous Recipe Country Chicken

Row 1: Cosmic Flyers-3 per set:
○ Toys 1-3 Cosmic Flyers
K-Mart 1994, $3-5 each.
Glows-in-the-Dark! 7" diameter.
Markings: "Humphery Flyer Made in USA" Label: ©1994 K-Mart Corp"

Row 2: Leaky Tiki Totems-3 per set:
○ Toy 1: Loony Lagoony
○ Toy 2: Golly Wally
○ Toy 3: Silly Spilly
K-Mart 1994, $4-5 each.
Squirters. They can stack on top of each other. Each squirter came with a sheet of 4 different peel-off face stickers.
Markings: "©1994 Peterson-Kennedy All Rights Reserved 1994 K-Mart Corp China"

Row 2: Puzzle Ornaments-3 per set:
○ Toy 4: Diamond Puzzle
○ Toy 5: Square Puzzle
○ Also: Round Puzzle

K-Mart 1994, $3-5 each.
Similar puzzles were distributed by Denny's.
Markings: "Kid's SM Meals"

Row 3: Kentucky Fried Chicken
○ Toy 1: KFC Flyer
○ Toy 2: KFC Truck
Kentucky Fried Chicken, $3-5 each.
Mini-disk has a 4" diameter.
Markings: "Humphrey Flyer Made in USA" and "yatming Made in Thailand" Truck decals: "KFC® Colonel's Kids"

Row 3: Cartoon Parade-5 per set:
○ Toy 3: Mighty Mouse Viewer
○ Toy 4: Porky Pig Viewer
○ Toy 5: Bugs Bunny Viewer-paper label missing
○ Also: Popeye Viewer and Woody Woodpecker Viewer
Lee's Famous Recipe Country Chicken 1993, $7-10 each.
Mini-viewers with cartoon strips.
Markings: "Hong Kong" Printed Decal: "Lee's Famous Recipe Country Chicken"

Little Caesar

Little Caesar & Long John Silver's
Row 1: Little Caesar-4 per set:
○ Toy 1: Little Caesar Squirter
○ Toy 2: Little Caesar Spinner
○ Toy 3: Little Caesar Ball
○ Toy 4: Little Caesar Popper
Little Caesar's Pizza, $1-3.
No Markings
Row 2: Little Caesar Caesar
○ Toy 1: Roll Em! Roll Em!
○ Toy 2: Blimp! Blimp!
○ Toy 3: Scuba! Scuba!
○ Toy 4: Pepperoni Flyer
○ Toy 5: Knock Down
○ Toy 6: Pan Pipes
○ Toy 7: Secret Ring
Little Caesar's Pizza 1992-5, $1-3 each.
Markings: "©1992 LCE Inc China"
Row 3: Fish Cards

○ Toy 1: Fish Cards
Long John Silver's 1989, $3-5
"Go Fish" card game.
Printed: "©1989 Long John Silver's All Rights Reserved"
Row 3: Go Fish Cars
○ Toys 2-4: Fish-Cars
Long John Silver's 1986, $7-10 each.
Peel-off stickers for details, various colors and stickers.
Markings: "Not intended for children under three"
Row 4: Once Upon a Forest-5 per set:
○ Toy 1: Abigail
○ Toy 2: Cornelius
○ Toy 3: Edgar
○ Toy 4: Michelle
○ Toy 5 & 6: Russell-2 different mold colors
Long John Silver's 1993, $4-6 each.
Straw Sliders, a cartoon motion picture.
Markings: "™ & ©1993 TCFFC"

Long John Silver's

Long John Silver's

Row 1: Sea Walkers-5 per set:
- Toy 1: Tommy
- Toy 2: Sylvia
- Toy 3: Sydney
- Toy 4: Quinn
- Toy 5: Captain Flint

Long John Silver's 1990, $4-6 each.
Each walker has a name disk to pull the critter into a walk.
No Markings

Row 2: Sea Watchers-3 per set:
- Toy 1: Pirates & Parrot-square prism
- Toy 2: Ship & Fish-linear prism
- Toy 3: Dolphin & Gator-radial prism

Long John Silver's 1990, $4-5 each.
Prism scopes.
Markings: "Long John Silver's Seafood Shoppes"

Row 2: Stone Protectors-7 per set:
- Toy 4: Angus the Soldier-white stone
- Toy 5: Clifford the Rock Climber-blue stone
- Toy 6: Cornelius the Samurai-green stone
- Toy 7: Chester the Wrestler-red stone
- Toy 8: Zok the Evil Leader-purple stone
- Toy 9: Zink the Horrible Hatchetman-pink stone
- Also: Maxwell the Accelerator

Long John Silver's 1994, $2-3 each.
About 1.5" tall, each with a different color stone. New Comic book characters.
Markings: "©ACE LDC China"

Row 3: Treasure Trolls-6 per set:
- Toys 1-6: No names

Long John Silver's 1993, $1-3 each.
Different colors of hair. Also distributed by Hardee's, Roy Rogers, Sonic, and Wal-Mart.
Markings: "China"

Row 4: Water Blasters-4 per set:
- Toy 1: Long John Silver
- Toy 2: Captain Flint
- Toy 3: Billy Bones
- Also: Ophelia Octopus

Long John Silver's 1990, $3-5 each.
Squirters.
Markings: "Copyright Long John Silver's Inc 1990 Made in China"

McDonald's

McDonald's
Row 1: 101 Dalmations-4 per set:
○ Toy 1: Cruella Deville
○ Toy 2: Lucky
○ Toy 3: Pongo
○ Toy 4: The Colonel & Sargent Tibbs
McDonald's 1992, $1-2 each.
A Disney cartoon motion picture.
Markings: "©Disney China"
Row 2: Alvin & The Chipmunks-4 per set & U-3:
○ Toy 1: Alvin with Guitar
○ Toy 2: Brittney with Jukebox
○ Toy 3: Simon with Movie Camera
○ Toy 4: Theodore with Rap Machine
○ Toy 5: U-3 Alvin at Jukebox
McDonald's 1990, $4-6 each.
Limited distribution, a TV cartoon series.
Markings: "® ©1990 Bagdasarian Prod China The Chipmunk®"
Rows 3 & 4: Animaniacs-8 per set & U-3:
○ Toy 1: Bicycle Built for Trio-also U-3
○ Toy 2: Dot's Ice Cream Wagon
○ Toy 3: Upside-down Yakko
○ Toy 4: Yakko Riding Ralph
○ Toy 5: Goodskate Goodfeathers
○ Toy 6: Slappy & Skippy's Chopper
○ Toy 7: Pinky & The Brain Mobile
○ Toy 8: Mindy & Buttons' Wild Ride
McDonald's 1994, $1-2 each.
A Warner Brothers cartoon series.
Markings: "™ & ©Warner Brothers China"

McDonald's

McDonald's
Row 1: Astrosniks 83-8 per set:
○ Toy 1: Skater
○ Toy 2: Sport
○ Toy 3: Scout with Flag
○ Toy 4: Robo
○ Toy 5: Thirsty
○ Toy 6: Laser
○ Toy 7: Astralia with Ice Cream Cone
○ Toy 8: Snikapotamus
McDonald's 1983, $3-7 each.
Limited distribution, all with the arches logo, from a TV cartoon series.
Markings: "©83 Bully-Figuren™ Astrosnik McDonald's® Hong Kong"
Row 2: Astrosniks 84-6 per set:
○ Toy 1: Racing Sled
○ Toy 2: Drill
○ Toy 3: Perfido Man
○ Toy 4: Commander
○ Toy 5: Copter-Rotobackpack
○ Toy 6: Skiing
McDonald's 1984, $3-7 each.
Limited distribution, all with the arches logo.
Markings: "©84 Bully-Figuren™ Astrosnik® McDonald's Hong Kong"
Row 3: Astrosniks 85-11 per set:
○ Toy 1: Pyramido
○ Toy 2: Perfido Man
○ Toy 3: Boy with Ice Cream Cone
○ Toy 4: Astrosnik on Rocket
○ Toy 5: Scout
○ Toy 6: Astrosnik with Headphones
○ Also: Laser, Commander, Snikapotamus, Robo, and Astralia
McDonald's 1985, $3-7 each.
Limited distribution, no arches logo on these.
Markings: "©83 Bully-Figuren ©Schaper Astrosniks™ Hong Kong"
Row 4: Attack Pack-4 per set:
○ Toy 1: Truck
○ Toy 2: Battle Bird
○ Toy 3: Sea Creature
○ Toy 4: Lunar Invader
McDonald's 1995, $1-2 each.
Markings: "Attack Pack (logo) Hot Wheels® ©1994 Mattel Inc China Chine"

McDonald's

McDonald's
Row 1: Back to the Future-4 per set:
○ Toy 1: Einstein's Traveling Train
○ Toy 2: Marty's Hoverboard
○ Toy 3: Vern's Junkmobile
○ Toy 4: Doc's Delorean-recalled
McDonald's 1992, $1-2 each. A motion picture.
Markings: "Back to the Future® ©1991 UCS & Amblin ©1991 McDonald's Corp China"
Row 2: Bambi-4 per set & 3 U-3s:
○ Toy 1: Owl
○ Toy 2: Bambi
○ Toy 3: Thumper
○ Toy 4: Flower
Row 3:
○ Toy 5: U-3 Bambi without Butterfly
○ Toy 6: U-3 Thumper
○ Toy 7: U-3 Bambi with Butterfly
McDonald's 1988, $1-3 each; U-3s, $5-7 each.
U-3s have no motion. A Disney cartoon motion picture.
Markings: "©Disney China"

McDonald's

Row 1: Barbie 91
- Toy 1: Hawaiian Fun
- Toy 2: Happy Birthday
- Toy 3: Ice Capades
- Toy 4: Prom
- Toy 5: My First Barbie
- Toy 6: Costume Ball
- Toy 7: Wedding Day Midge
- Toy 8: All American

McDonald's 1991, $3-5 each.
Markings: "Made for McDonald's ©Mattel Inc Made in China"

Row 2: Barbie 92-8 per set:
- Toy 1: My First Ballerina
- Toy 2: Sparkle Eyes
- Toy 3: Rappin' & Rockin'
- Toy 4: Birthday Surprise
- Toy 5: Sun Sensation
- Toy 6: Snap 'N Play
- Toy 7: Rollerblade
- Toy 8: Rose Bride

McDonald's 1992, $3-4 each.
Markings: "Made for McDonald's ©1992 Mattel Inc Made in China"

Row 3: Barbie 93-8 per set & U-3:
- Toy 1: My First Ballerina
- Toy 2: Secret Hearts
- Toy 3: Twinkle Lights
- Toy 4: Hollywood Hair
- Toy 5: U-3 Ball
- Toy 6: Western Stampin'
- Toy 7: Birthday Party
- Toy 8: Romantic Bride
- Toy 9: Paint 'n Dazzle

McDonald's 1993, $2-3 each; U-3, $4-5
Markings: "Made for McDonald's ©Mattel Inc China"

McDonald's

McDonald's
Row 1: Barbie 94-8 per set & U-3:
○ Toy 1: Bicyclin'
○ Toy 2: Jewel & Glitter Shani
○ Toy 3: Camp Barbie
○ Toy 4: Camp Teresa
○ Toy 5: U-3 Ball
○ Toy 6: Locket Surprise-also African-American
○ Toy 7: Locket Surprise Ken-also English
○ Toy 8: Jewel & Glitter Bride
○ Toy 9: Bridesmaid Skipper
McDonald's 1994, $2-3 each; #5 & 6 African-Americans, $5-7 each.
Markings: "Made for McDonald's ©Mattel Inc China"
Row 2: Basic 4-4 per set & U-3:
○ Toy 1: Slugger
○ Toy 2: Otis
○ Toy 3: Milly
○ Toy 4: Ruby
○ Toy 5: U-3 Dunkan
McDonald's 1993, $1-2 each.
Markings: "©1993 McDonald's Corp China"
Row 3: Batman-4 per set & 1:
○ Toy 1: Batmobile
○ Toy 2: Catwoman in Cat Coupe
○ Toy 3: Penguine in Umbrella
○ Toy 4: Batman Press & Go Car
○ Toy 5: Batman Returns Minidisk-drink cover
McDonald's 1992, $1-3 each.
A motion picture.
Markings: "©1991 DC Comics China"

McDonald's

McDonald's
Row 1: Batman the Animated Series-4 per set & U-3:
○ Toy 1: Batman with Removable Cape
○ Toy 2: Batgirl
○ Toy 3: Catwoman & Leopard
○ Toy 4: The Riddler
○ Toy 5: Poison Ivy
○ Toy 6: Robin
○ Toy 7: Two-Face
○ Toy 8: The Joker
○ Also: U-3 Batman with Attached Cape
McDonald's 1993, $1-3 each.
TV cartoon series.
Markings: "©1993 DC China"
Row 2: Behind the Scenes-4 per set:
○ Toy 1: Animation Wheel
○ Toy 2: Balance Builders-multipieces
○ Toy 3: Rub & Draw Templates
○ Toy 4: Rainbow Viewer
McDonald's 1992, $1 each.
Balance builders also distributed by Dairy Queen.
Markings: "©1992 McDonald's Corp China"
Row 3: Berenstain Bears-4 per set & 2 U-3s:
○ Toy 1: Papa & Wheelbarrow
○ Toy 2: Mama & Cart
○ Toy 3: Brother & Scooter
○ Toy 4: Sister & Wagon
○ Toy 5: U-3 Papa-no flocking
○ Toy 6: U-3 Mama-no flocking
McDonald's 1987, $2-3 each; U-3's, $5-7 each.
Markings: "©1986 S&J Berenstain China"
Row 4: Big Foot-4 per set:
○ Toy 1: Ford Pickup
○ Toy 2: Ford Bronco
○ Toy 3: Shuttle Ford
○ Toy 4: MS Ford Pickup
McDonald's 1987, $2-4 each.
Each of the four models came in different colors, with & without the arches logo, making a total of sixteen different cars.
Markings: "Bigfoot China"

McDonald's

McDonald's

Row 1: Bobby's World-4 per set & U-3:
○ Toy 1: Innertube/Submarine
○ Toy 2: Wagon/Race Car
○ Toy 3: Skates/Roller Coaster
Row 2:
○ Toy 4: 3 Wheeler/Spaceship
○ Toy 5: U-3 Innertube-squirter
McDonald's 1994, $1-2 each; U-3, $3-4 A TV cartoon series.
Markings: "©/™ FCN 94 China"
Row 3: Cabbage Patch 92-5 per set & U-3:
○ Toy 1: All Dressed Up
○ Toy 2: Fun on Ice
○ Toy 3: Tiny Dancer
○ Toy 4: Holiday Dreamer
○ Toy 5: Holiday Pageant
○ Toy 6: U-3 Ribbons & Bows
McDonald's 1992, $1-2 each; U-3, $5.
Markings: "©1992 OAA China"
Row 4: Cabbage Patch 94-4 per set & U-3:
○ Toy 1: Abigail Lynn
○ Toy 2: Mimi Kristina
○ Toy 3: Michelle Elyse
○ Toy 4: Kimberly Katherine
○ Toy 5: U-3 Sarajane
McDonald's 1994, $1-2 each; U-3, $3-5.
Markings: "©1994 OAA Inc China"

McDonald's

McDonald's

Row 1: Chip 'n Dales Rescue Rangers-6 per set & 2 U-3s:
- Toy 1: Chip's Whirley-Copter
- Toy 2: Dale's Roto Roadster
- Toy 3: Gadget's Rescue Racer
- Toy 4: Monteray Jack's Propel-A-Phone
- Toy 5: U-3 Gadget in Rockin' Rider
- Toy 6: U-3 Chip in Rockin' Racer

McDonald's 1990, $2-4 each.
Disney TV cartoon series.
Markings: "©Disney China RR (logo)"

Row 2: Dink the Little Dinosaur-6 per set:
- Toy 1: Flapper
- Toy 2: Shyler
- Toy 3: Dink
- Toy 4: Amber
- Toy 5: Crusty
- Toy 6: Scat-solid PVC

McDonald's 1990, $5-6 each.
Limited distribution, finger puppets.
Markings: "©1989 Ruby-Spears Inc China"

Row 3: Dinosaurs-6 per set & U-3:
- Toy 1: Grandma Ethyl
- Toy 2: Baby Sinclair
- Toy 3: Fran Sinclair-2 pieces
- Toy 4: Earl Sinclair
- Toy 5: Charlene Sinclair
- Toy 6: Robbie Sinclair
- Toy 7: U-3 Baby

McDonald's 1993, $1-2 each; U-3, $2-3.
A Disney TV series.
Markings: "©Disney China"

Row 4: Drive Thru Crew-4 per set:
- Toy 1: McNugget Speedster
- Toy 2: Milk Carton Zoomer
- Also: Egg Roadster and Hamburger Ketchup Racer

McDonald's 1990, $4-6 each.
Limited distribution.
Markings: "©1989 McDonald's Corp China"

Row 4: Ducktales 87-4 per set & U-3:
- Toy 3: Spy Glass
- Toy 4: Magnifying Glass
- Toy 5: Watch
- Toy 6: Quaker Whistle-also sold retail
- Also: U-3 Magic Motion Map

McDonald's 1987, $3-4 each; U-3, $5.
TV cartoon series.
Markings: "©1987 McDonald's Corp Made in W Germany"

McDonald's

Row 1: Disneyland 40th Anniversary Parade-8 per set & U-3:
- Toy 1: Simba in The Lion King Celebration
- Toy 2: Brer Bear on Splash Mountain
- Toy 3: U-3 Winnie the Pooh on Big Thunder Mountain Railroad-also with viewer
- Toy 4: Aladdin & Jasmine at Aladdin's Oasis

Row 2:
- Toy 5: Mickey Mouse on Space Mountain
- Toy 6: Roger Rabbit in Benny in Mickey's Toontown
- Toy 7: King Louie on the Jungle Cruise
- Toy 8: Peter Pan in Fantasmia

McDonald's 1995, $1-2 each. Viewers.
Markings: "©Disney-Amblin China Chine"

McDonald's

Row 1: Ducktales 88-4 per set & U-3:
- Toy 1: Webby on Tricycle-2 pieces
- Toy 2: Scrooge McDuck in Car-2 pieces
- Toy 3: Huey, Dewey & Louie on Jet Ski
- Toy 4: Launchpad in His Airplane
- Toy 5: U-3 Huey

McDonald's 1988, $3-5 each; U-3, $6-7. Limited distribution.
Markings: "©1987 Disney China"

Row 2: Flintstone Kids-4 per set & U-3:
- Toy 1: Wilma & Dragon
- Toy 2: Betty & Pteradactyl
- Toy 3: Fred & Crocasaurus
- Toy 4: Barney & Mastodon
- Toy 5: U-3 Dino

McDonald's 1988, $5-10 each; U-3, $12-20. Limited distribution, two pieces each (except U-3). TV cartoon series by Hanna-Barbera.
Markings: "©1988 H-B Prod Inc China"

Row 3: Flintstones-5 per set & U-3:
- Toy 1: Fred & Bedrock Bow-O-Rama-3 pieces
- Toy 2: Barney & Fossil Fill-Up-3 pieces
- Toy 3: Pebbles, Dino & Toy-S-Aurus-2 pieces

Row 4:
- Toy 4: Wilma & The Flintstone House-2 pieces
- Toy 5: Betty & Bamm-Bamm & Roc Donald's-3 pieces
- Toy 6: U-3 Rocking Dino

McDonald's 1994, $1-2 each; U-3, $3-5 each.
A motion picture, two units each-a building to "garage" the vehicles. Details are peel-off stickers.
Markings: "©UCS & Amblin China"

McDonald's

McDonald's
Row 1: Fraggle Rock-4 per set & 2 U-3s:
○ Toy 1: Red in Radish Car
○ Toy 2: Wimbly & Goober in Cucumber Car
○ Toy 3: Gobo in Carrot Car
○ Toy 4: Mokey in Eggplant Car
○ Toy 5: U-3 Gobo with Carrot
○ Toy 6: U-3 Red with Radish
McDonald's 1988, $1-2 each; U-3s, $3-4 each.
Jim Henson's Puppet characters TV series.
Markings: "©Henson Associates China"
Row 2: Fry Benders-4 per set & U-3:
○ Toy 1: Grand Slam
○ Toy 2: Freestyle
○ Toy 3: Roadie
○ Toy 4: Froggy
○ Toy 5: U-3 Tunes
McDonald's 1989, $3-4 each; U-3, $5.

Three pieces each (except U-3).
Markings: "©1989 McDonald's China"
Row 3: Fun with Food-4 per set:
○ Toy 1: McNugget Guys
○ Toy 2: Hamburger Guy
○ Toy 3: French Fry Guy
○ Toy 4: Soft Drink Cup & Lid Guy
McDonald's 1989, $2-3 each.
Multipieces each.
Markings: "©1988 McDonald's Corporation China"
Row 4: Funny Fry Friends-8 per set & 2 U-3s:
○ Toy 1: Hoops
○ Toy 2: Matey
○ Toy 3: Tracker
○ Toy 4: Sweet Cuddles
○ Toy 5: Rollin' Rocker
(Continued in next photo)

McDonald's

McDonald's

Row 1: Funny Fry Friends-8 per set & 2 U-3s-(continued from previous photo):
○ Toy 6: ZZZ's
○ Toy 7: Gadzooks
○ Toy 8: Too Tall
○ Toy 9: U-3 Cowgirl
○ Toy 10: U-3 Indian
McDonald's 1989, $3-5 each.
Three pieces each.
Markings: "©1989 McDonald's Corporation China"
Row 2: Garfield-4 per set & 2 U-3s:
○ Toy 1: In 4-Wheeler
○ Toy 2: On Skateboard
○ Toy 3: On Scooter
○ Toy 4: On Motorcycle with Odie in Sidecar
○ Toy 5: U-3 On Skateboard
○ Toy 6: U-3 On Skates
McDonald's 1989, $3-4 each; U-3s, $4-6 each.
Limited distribution.
Markings: "©1988 McDonald's China"
Row 3: Ghostbusters-6 per set:
○ Toy 1: Stay Puft Marshmallow Man Pencil Sharpener
○ Toy 2: Ghostbusters Eraser
○ Toy 3: Slimer Pencil Topper
○ Also: Pencil, Pencil case, Notepad, Ruler
McDonald's 1987, $3-5 each.
Markings: "©1984 Columbia Pictures Industries Inc ©198 Columbia Pictures Television A Division of CPT Holdings"
Row 3: Gravedale High-4 per set & U-3:
○ Toy 4: Sid (The Invisible Kid)
○ Toy 5: Frankentyke
○ Toy 6: Cleofatra-also U-3
○ Toy 7: Vinnie Stoker
McDonald's 1990, $4-5 each.
Limited distribution.
Markings: "©1991 NBC Made in China"
Row 4: Halloween McNugget Buddies-6 per set & U-3:
○ Toy 1: McNuggula
○ Toy 2: McBoo McNugget-also U-3
○ Toy 3: Pumpking McNugget
○ Toy 4: Monster McNugget
○ Toy 5: Mummie McNugget
○ Toy 6: Witchie McNugget
McDonald's 1992, $2-3 each.
Markings: "©1992 McDonald's Corp Made in China"

McDonald's

McDonald's
Row 1: Happy Birthday-15 per set:
- Toy 1: Ronald McDonald™
- Toy 2: Barbie™-recalled
- Toy 3: Hot Wheels™
- Toy 4: ET®
- Toy 5: Sonic The Hedgehog™

Row 2:
- Toy 6: The Berenstain Bears™
- Toy 7: Tonka®-two pieces
- Toy 8: Cabbage Patch Kids®
- Toy 9: 101 Dalmatians
- Toy 10: Disney's The Little Mermaid®

Row 3:
- Toy 11: Jim Henson's Muppet Babies™
- Toy 12: Peanuts®
- Toy 13: Tiny Toons®
- Toy 14: Looney Tunes™
- Toy 15: The Happy Meal® Guys

McDonald's 1995, $1-2 each.
All have motion and hook together.
Markings: "©1994 McDonald's Corp China"

Row 4: Hook-4 per set & U-3:
- Toy 1: Peter Pan-3 pieces
- Toy 2: Rufio Squirter-also U-3
- Toy 3: Wind-Up Mermaid
- Toy 4: Hook-2 pieces

McDonald's 1992, $1-2 each.
A motion picture.
Markings: "©1991 Tri-Star Pictures Inc ©1991 McDonald's Corp"

McDonald's

McDonald's
Row 1: Hot Wheels 91-8 per set & U-3:
○ Toy 1: '55 Chevy
○ Toy 2: '63 Vette
○ Toy 3: '57 T-Bird
○ Toy 4: Camaro Z28
○ Toy 5: '55 Chevy
Row 2:
○ Toy 6: '63 Vette
○ Toy 7: '57 T-Bird
○ Toy 8: Camaro Z28
○ Toy 9: U-3 Wrench & Hammer
McDonald's 1991, $2-3 each; U-3, $4-5.
Markings: "Hot Wheels® ©Mattel Inc 1978 Malaysia"

Row 3: Hot Wheels 93-8 per set & U-3:
○ Toy 1: McDonald's Funny Car
○ Toy 2: Quaker State Racer
○ Toy 3: McDonald's Thunderbird
○ Toy 4: Hot Wheels Funny Car
○ Toy 5: McDonald's Dragster
Row 4:
○ Toy 6: Hot Wheels Camaro
○ Toy 7: Duracell Racer
○ Toy 8: Hot Wheels Dragster
○ Toy 9: U-3 Wrench & Hammer
McDonald's 1993, $1-2 each; U-3, $4-5.
Markings: "Hot Wheels ©1993 Mattel Inc"

McDonald's

McDonald's
Row 1: Hot Wheels 94-8 per set & U-3:
- Toy 1: Bold Eagle
- Toy 2: Black Cat
- Toy 3: Flame Rider
- Toy 4: Gas Hog
- Toy 5: Turbine 4-2

Row 2:
- Toy 6: 2-Cool
- Toy 7: Street Shocker
- Toy 8: X21J Cruiser
- Toy 9: U-3 fast Forward Vehicle

McDonald's 1994, $ 1-2 each; U-3, $3.
Markings: "©1994 Mattel Inc Hot Wheels China"

Row 3: Jungle Book-4 per set & 2 U-3s:
- Toy 1: Shere Khan
- Toy 2: Kaa
- Toy 3: King Louie
- Toy 4: Baloo
- Toy 5: U-3 Junior
- Toy 6: U-3 Mowgli

McDonald's 1989, $2-3 each; U-3s, $5-8 each.
A Disney cartoon motion picture.
Markings: "©Disney China"

Row 4: Kisseyfur-8 per set:
- Toy 1: Gus the Bear
- Toy 2: Floyd the Alligator
- Toy 3: Jolene the Alligator
- Toy 4: Kisseyfur
- Toy 5: Lennie the Warthog-flocked
- Toy 6: Toot the Beaver-flocked
- Toy 7: Behonie the Rabbit-flocked
- Toy 8: Duane the Pig-flocked

McDonald's 1987, $4-6 each.
Limited distribution.
Markings: "©1985 Phil Mendez Made in China"

McDonald's

McDonald's

Row 1: Little Mermaid-4 per set:
○ Toy 1: Prince Eric & Sebastian-2 pieces
○ Toy 2: Ariel with Seahorse
○ Toy 3: Flounder Squirter-marked: "©Disney"
○ Toy 4: Ursula the Sea Witch
McDonald's 1989, $2-3 each.
A Disney cartoon motion picture. Little Mermaid toys were also distributed by Burger King.
Markings: "©Disney China"

Row 2: Looney Tunes Quack-Up Cars- 4 per set & U-3:
○ Toy 1: Taz in Tornado Tracker
○ Toy 2: Daffy in Splittin' Sportster
○ Toy 3: Porky in Ghost Catcher
○ Toy 4: Bugs in Super Stretch Limo-also in red
○ Toy 5: U-3 Bugs in Swingin' Sedan-also in orange
McDonald's 1993, $1-2 each; orange, $4-5 each. With the color change, there is a total of seven collectibles here. The orange Bugs' cars had limited distribution.
Markings: "™ & ©92 Warner Bros China"

Row 3: M Squad-4 per set & U-3:
○ Toy 1: Spynoculars
○ Toy 2: Spycoder
○ Toy 3: Spytracker/Watch/Compass
○ Toy 4: Spy Stamper/Calculator
○ Toy 5: U-3 Watch-no compass
McDonald's 1992, $1-2 each.
Markings: "©1992 McDonald's Corp Made in China"

Row 4: Mac Tonight
○ Toys 1-3 Mac Tonight
McDonald's 1991, $5-7 each.
Some of these figurines were distributed to some customers in the restaurants. Others were sold in retail stores.
Markings: "©1998 McDonald's Corp Button Up Company China"

McDonald's

McDonald's
Row 1: MacTonight-6 per set & U-3:
○ Toy 1: Off Roader
○ Toy 2: Motorscooter
○ Toy 3: Porsche
○ Toy 4: Surf Ski-with & without wheels
○ Toy 5: Motorcycle
○ Toy 6: Airplane-with blue or black glasses
○ Toy 7: U-3 Skateboard
McDonald's 1991, $3-5 each; U-3, $4-6.
Limited distribution.
Markings: "©1988 McDonald's China"
Row 2: Magic School Bus-4 per set & U-3:
○ Toy 1: Undersea Adventure Game
○ Toy 2: In the Solar System
○ Toy 3: Collector Card Kit
○ Toy 4: Geo-Fossil Finder
○ Toy 5: U-3 Undersea Adventure Game
McDonald's 1994, $1 each.
PBS TV series.
Markings: "©1994 Scholastic Inc China"
Row 3: Making Movies-4 per set & U-3:
○ Toy 1: Sound Effects Machine-also U-3
○ Toy 2: Movie Camera
○ Toy 3: Director's Megaphone
○ Toy 4: Clapboard
McDonald's 1994, $1 each.
Markings: "©1993 McDonald's Corp China"
Row 4: McDonald's Airport-6 per set & 2 U-3s:
○ Toy 1: Ronald's Seaplane
○ Toy 2: Fry Guy Flyer
○ Toy 3: Birdie Bent Wing Blazer
○ Toy 4: Grimace Ace Biplane
(continued in next photograph)

McDonald's

McDonald's
Row 1: McDonald's Airport-(continued from previous photograph):
○ Toy 5: Fry Guy Hello Copter
○ Toy 6: Big Mac Helicopter-dated 1982
○ Toy 7: U-3 Grimace Smiling Shuttle
○ Toy 8: U-3 Fry Guy Friendly Flyer
McDonald's 1986, $3-5 each; U-3, $2-3 each.
Various colors for each.
Markings: "©1986 McDonald's Made in USA"
Row 2: McDonald's Bedtime-1 figurine:
○ Toy 1: Ronald
McDonald's 1988, $2-3.
Limited distribution.
Marking: "Ronald McDonald® ©1988 McDonald's Corp Made in China"
Row 2: McDonald's Carnival-4 per set & U-3:
○ Toy 2: Ronald on Carousel
○ Toy 3: Birdie on Swing
Row 3:
○ Toy 4: Hamburgular on Ferris Wheel
○ Toy 5: Grimace on Turn-Around
○ Toy 6: U-3 Grimace
McDonald's 1990, $3-4 each; U-3, $5. Multipieces.
Markings: "©1990 McDonald's China"
Row 4: McDonald's Circus Parade-4 per set:
○ Toy 1: Ronald Ringmaster
○ Toy 2: Bareback Rider Birdie
○ Toy 3: Elephant Trainer Fry Guy
○ Toy 4: Grimace Playing Calliope
McDonald's 1989, $4-6 each.
Limited distribution.
Markings: "©1989 McDonald's Corp China"

McDonald's

McDonald's

Row 1: McDonald's Connectibles and Linkables-4 per set:
- Toy 1: Grimace in Wagon
- Toy 2: Ronald in Soap Box Racer
- Toy 3: Birdie on Tricycle
- Toy 4: Hamburgular in Airplane

McDonald's 1991 & 1993, $3-4 each.
Limited distribution, the same set was given out with different names at different times.
Markings: "©1990 McDonald's Corp China"

Row 2: McDonald's Crazy Vehicles-4 per set:
- Toy 1: Ronald
- Toy 2: Grimace
- Toy 3: Hamburgular
- Toy 4: Birdie

McDonald's 1990, $3-5 each.
Limited distribution, three pieces each.
Markings: "©1990 McDonald's Corp China"

Row 3: McDonald's Design-O-Saurs-4 per set & 2 U-3s:
- Toy 1: Fry Guy on McBronto
- Toy 2: Hamburgular on McTops
- Toy 3: U-3 Team McDonald's
- Toy 4: U-3 Happy Taxi
- Also: Grimace on McDactyl and Ronald on McRex

McDonald's 1987, $2-3 each.
Various colors.
Markings: "©1987 McDonald's® Corporation Made in USA"

Row 4: McDonald's Fast Macs-5 per set:
- Toy 1: Hamburgular
- Toy 2: Big Mac
- Toy 3: Ronald
- Toy 4: Birdie
- Also: Mayor McCheese in Sun Cruiser

McDonald's 1984, $2-4 each; Mayor McCheese, $4-5.
Markings: "McDonald's Corp ©1984 the Ertle Co® Dyersville Iowa USA Made in Hong Kong"

Row 4: McDonald's Feeling Good-2 figurines:
- Toy 5: U-3 Grimace in Tub
- Toy 6: U-3 Fry Guy on Duck

McDonald's 1985, $4-5 each.
Other items are not toys.
Markings: "©1984 ©McDonald's Made in USA"

McDonald's

McDonald's

Row 1: McDonald's Flyers-4 per set:
- Toy 1: Big Mac
- Toy 2: Ronald
- Also: Birdie & Hamburgular

McDonald's 1994, $1 each.
Markings: "Safety tested for children 3 and over"

Row 2: McDonald's Friendly Skies-2 per set:
- Toy 1: Ronald-also in white airplane
- Toy 2: Grimace

McDonald's 1992, $5-10 each.
Only distributed on selected United Air Lines Flights.
Markings: "©1991 McDonald's Corp ©1991 United Air Lines Inc China"

Row 2: McDonald's Good Morning-2 per set:
- Toy 1: Clock
- Toy 2: Comb

McDonald's 1990, $1-3 each.
Markings: "©1989 McDonald's Corp China"

Row 3: McDonald's Little Engineer-
5 per set & 2 U-3s
- Toy 1: Ronald
- Toy 2: Fry Guy
- Toy 3: Birdie
- Toy 4: Fry Girl
- Toy 5: Grimace
- Toy 6: U-3 Fry Guy Team McDonald's-also in yellow
- Toy 7: U-3 Grimace in Happy Taxi-also in aqua

McDonald's 1986 #1-4, $3-5 each; #5, $5, #6 & 7, $2-4 each.
Limited distribution, each had peel-off stickers.
Markings: under wheels-Made by Monogram Models

Row 4: McDonald's Movables-6 per set:
- Toy 1: Birdie
- Toy 2: Captain
- Toy 3: Ronald
- Toy 4: Professor
- Toy 5: Hamburgular
- Toy 6: Fry Girl

McDonald's 1988, $3-5 each.
Limited distribution.
Markings: "©1988 McDonald's Corp Made in China"

McDonald's

McDonald's
Row 1: McDonald's Olympic Sports Badges-
per set:
○ Toy 1: Ronald
○ Toy 2: Birdie
○ Toy 3: Hamburgular
○ Toy 4: Grimace
○ Toy 5: Fry Girl
○ Toy 6: McCosmo
McDonald's 1988, $3-4 each.
Also distributed in McDonald's Europe.
Markings: "©1988 McDonald's Corp"
Row 2: McDonald's Sailors-4 per set & 2 U-3s:
○ Toy 1: Ronald-in Airboat (missing boat)
○ Toy 2: Grimace in Submarine
○ Toy 3: Hamburgular in Pirate Boat
○ Toy 4: U-3 Fry Guy on Inner Tube
○ Also: Fry Kids in Ferry and U-3 Grimace on Speed Boat
McDonald's 1987, $3-4 each.
Limited distribution.
Markings: "©1987 McDonald's Corp"

Row 3: McDonald's Turbo Macs-
5 per set & U-3:
○ Toy 1: Birdie
○ Toy 2: Ronald
○ Toy 3: Big Mac
○ Toy 4: Hamburgular
○ Toy 5: Grimace
○ Toy 6: U-3 Ronald
McDonald's 1985, $4-5 each; U-3, $5-7.
Limited distribution in USA, also given out in McDonald's Canada.
Markings: "McDonald's ©1985 Macau"
Row 4: McDonald's Water Games-
4 per set & U-3:
○ Toy 1: Birdie
○ Toy 2: Ronald
○ Toy 3: Hamburgular
○ Toy 4: Grimace
○ Toy 5: U-3 Grimace
McDonald's 1992, $5-6 each.
Limited distribution.
Markings: McDonald's logo

McDonald's

Row 1: McDonald's United Airlines
○ Toy 1: Building
McDonald's 1994, $5-10
Came with small airplane, peel-off stickers, door opens. Given out on selected United Airlines Flights.
Markings: "©1994 McDonald's Corp ©United Airlines Inc China"

Row 2: McDonaldland Junction-4 per set:
○ Toy 1: Steam Engine-(Ronald missing)-also in blue
○ Toy 2: Coach with Birdie-also in pink
○ Toy 3: Flat Car-(Fry Kids missing)-also in white
○ Toy 4: Caboose with Grimace-also in purple
McDonald's 1983, $3-5 each.
Limited distribution.
Markings: "©1982 McDonald's Corporation Made in USA"

McDonald's

Row 1: McDonaldland (Tricycles)-4 per set:
○ Toy 1: Ronald
○ Toy 2: Birdie
○ Toy 3: Hamburgular
○ Toy 4: Grimace
McDonald's 1991, $3-5 each.
Limited distribution.
Markings: "©1989 Simon Mkt ©1989 McDonald's Corp"

Row 2: McDonaldland Band-8 per set:
○ Toy 1: Engine Ronald
○ Toy 2: Kazoo Birdie
○ Toy 3: Ronald Pan Pipes
○ Toy 4: Hamburgular Siren
○ Toy 5: Fry Girl Trumpet
○ Toy 6: Fry Guy Boat
○ Toy 7: Saxophone Grimace
○ Also: Harmonica
McDonald's 1986, $1 each.
Limited distribution, also sold retail.

Markings: "©1986 McDonald's Corporation Made in USA"

Row 3: McNugget Buddies-10 per set & 2 U-3s:
○ Toy 1: Mailman
○ Toy 2: Policeman
○ Toy 3: Scuba Diver
○ Toy 4: Drum Major
○ Toy 5: Popcorn Vender
○ Toy 6: Tennis Player

Row 4:
○ Toy 7: Cowpoke
○ Toy 8: Fireman
○ Toy 9: Rock Star
○ Toy 10: Camper
○ Toy 11: U-3 Daisy
○ Toy 12: U-3 Slugger
McDonald's 1988, $3-5 each.
Three pieces each.
Markings: "©1988 McDonald's Corp China"

McDonald's

McDonald's

Row 1: Mickey & Friends Epcot Center-per set:
- Toy 1: Mickey in USA
- Toy 2: Minnie in Japan
- Toy 3: Daisy in Germany
- Toy 4: Donald in Mexico
- Toy 5: Goofy in Norway
- Toy 6: Dale in Morocco
- Toy 7: Chip in China
- Toy 8: Pluto in France

McDonald's 1994, $2-4 each.
Adventure at Walt Disney World.
Markings: "©Disney China"

Row 2: Mickey's Birthday Land-per set & 4 U-3s:
- Toy 1: Mickey's Roadster
- Toy 2: Minnie's Convertible
- Toy 3: Pluto's Rumbler
- Toy 4: Goofy's Sport Coupe
- Toy 5: Donald's Engine
- Toy 6: U-3 Mickey's Car
- Toy 7: U-3 Minnies' Car
- Toy 8: U-3 Goofy's Car-also in green
- Toy 9: U-3 Donald's Car-also in blue

McDonald's 1988, $2-3 each; U-3s, $5-7 each.
U-3s have a face decal on the hood or roofs (not shown in picture, sorry).
Markings: "©Disney China"

Row 3: Mighty Mini-4 per set & U-3:
- Toy 1: Pocket Pickup
- Toy 2: Li'l Classic T Bird
- Toy 3: Cargo Climber Van
- Toy 4: Dune Buster
- Toy 5: U-3 Pocket Pickup

McDonald's 1990, $2-4 each.
Limited distribution, Wind-ups.
Markings: "McDonald's Corp China"

Row 4: Mini-Streex-8 per set:
- Toy 1: Black Arrow
- Toy 2: Blade Burner
- Toy 3: Flame Out
- Toy 4: Hot Shock
- Toy 5: Night Shadow
- Toy 6: Quick Flash
- Toy 7: Racer Tracer
- Toy 8: Turbo Flyer

McDonald's 1992, $1-3 each.
The correct launcher is behind each Mini-Streex.
Markings: "©1991 McDonald's Corp Streex is a Registered Trademark of Mattel Inc Made in China"

McDonald's

McDonald's
Row 1: Mix-Em Up Monsters-4 per set:
○ Toy 1: Bibble
○ Toy 2: Gropple
○ Toy 3: Corkle
○ Toy 4: Thugger
McDonald's 1989, $1-3 each.
Also distributed by Avon.
Markings: "Current Inc"
Row 2: Muppet Babies 87-4 per set & 2 U-3s:
○ Toy 1: Kermit
○ Toy 2: Miss Piggy
○ Toy 3: Gonzo
○ Toy 4: Fozzie
○ Toy 5: U-3 Kermit
○ Toy 6: U-3 Miss Piggy
McDonald's 1986, $4-5 each.
Jim Henson's Muppet characters.
Markings: "©1986 McDonald's China"
Row 3: Muppet Babies 90-4 per set:
○ Toy 1: Gonzo
○ Toy 2: Kermit
○ Toy 3: Miss Piggy
○ Toy 4: Fozzie
McDonald's 1990, $3-5 each.
Limited distribution.
Markings: "©1990 McDonald's Corp China"
Row 4: Mystery of the Lost Arches-4 per set:
○ Toy 1: Phone/Periscope
○ Toy 2: Cassette/Magnifier
○ Toy 3: Flashlight/Telescope
○ Toy 4: Magic Lens Camera-also U-3-recalled
McDonald's 1991, $1 each.
Markings: "©1991 McDonald's Corp China"

McDonald's

McDonald's
Row 1: Muppet Workshop-4 per set:
Toy 1: Bird
Toy 2: Dog
Toy 3: Monster
Toy 4: What-Not-also U-3
McDonald's 1994, $1 each.
Two removable pieces each, 4" to 6" tall.
Markings: "©Jim Henson Productions Inc China"
Row 2: New Archies-6 per set:
Toy 1: Archie
Toy 2: Betty
Toy 3: Moose
Toy 4: Jughead
Toy 5: Veronica
Toy 6: Reggie
McDonald's 1987, $4-6 each.
Limited distribution.
Markings: "©1987 ACP Made in China ©1988 McDonald's Corp"
Row 3: New Food Changeables to Dinosaurs-8 per set & 2 U-3s:
○ Toy 1: Happy-Meal-O-Don
○ Toy 2: McDino Cone
○ Toy 3: Quarter Pounder Cheese-O-Saur
○ Toy 4: McNuggers-O-Saurus
○ Toy 5: Mac-O-Saurus Rex
Row 4:
○ Toy 6: Tri-Shake-Atops
○ Toy 7: Hot-Cakes-O-Dactyl
○ Toy 8: Fry-Ceratops
○ Toy 9: U-3 Small Fry-Ceratops
○ Toy 10: U-3 Bronto Cheeseburger
McDonald's 1991, $2-4 each; U-3s, $4-5 each.
Transformers from food to dinos.
Markings: "©1990 McDonald's Corp"

McDonald's

McDonald's
Row 1: New Food Changeables to Robots-12-per set & U-3:
○ Toy 1: Chicken McNuggets
○ Toy 2: Ice Cream Cone
○ Toy 3: Shake-circular opening
○ Toy 4: Quarter Pounder
○ Toy 5: Small White Box Fries
○ Toy 6: Cheeseburger
○ Toy 7: Big Mac
Row 2:
○ Toy 8: Hot Cakes
○ Toy 9: Egg McMuffin
○ Toy 10: Large Fries-in red box-also blue robot
○ Toy 11: Shake-splitting lengthwise
○ Toy 12: Quarter Pounder Box
○ Toy 13: U-3 Puzzle Cube: Birdie, Hamburgular, Grimace, and McCosmo
McDonald's 1987, 1988, $1-3 each; U-3, $5.
Various pieces were distributed with several offers with several dates.
Markings: "©1987 McDonald's Corporation China"
Row 3: Oliver & Company-4 per set:
○ Toy 1: Oliver
○ Toy 2: Francis
○ Toy 3: Georgette
○ Toy 4: Dodger
McDonald's 1988, $1-2 each.
Finger puppets, a Disney cartoon motion picture.
Markings: "©1988 Disney China"
Row 4: Peanuts-4 per set & 2 U-3s:
○ Toy 1: Snoopy's Hay Hauler
○ Toy 2: Linus' Milk Mover
○ Toy 3: Charlie Brown's Seed Bag 'n' Tiller
○ Toy 4: Lucy's Apple Cart
○ Toy 5: U-3 Snoopy
○ Toy 6: U-3 Charlie Brown
McDonald's 1989, $1-3 each; U-3s, $5-7 each.
Three pieces each, except U-3s.
No Markings

McDonald's

cDonald's
ow 1: Piggsbury Pigs-4 per set:
 Toy 1: Portly & Pig Head on Cycle with Side Car
 Toy 2: Rembrant in Barnyard Hot Rod
 Toy 3: Huff & Puff on Catapult-2 pieces
 Toy 4: Piggy & Quackers on Crate Racer
cDonald's 1990, $4-7 each.
nited distribution.
arkings: "™/©1990 Fox Ch's Net Inc Made in China"
ow 2: Playmobile
 Toy 1: Sheriff
 Toy 2: Indian
 Toy 3: Horse
 Toy 4: Girl-missing Umbrella & Luggage
 Toy 5: Farmer-missing rake
cDonald's 1982, $7-20 each.
e toys were recalled after complaints of small parts.
der-3 toys were then distributed.

Markings: "©1974 b (logo) Geobra"
Row 3: Polly Pocket-4 per set:
○ Toy 1: Bracelet-girls on see-saw
○ Toy 2: Watch-gears turn, girls riding the watch hands
○ Toy 3: Locket-girl swings
○ Toy 4: Ring-petals turn
McDonald's 1995, $1-2.
Markings: "Polly Pocket (logo) ©1994 Blue Bird Toys China Chine"
Row 4: Potato Head Kids-8 per set:
○ Toy 1: Slick
○ Toy 2: Sabrina
○ Toy 3: Spike
○ Toy 4: Tulip
○ Also: Slugger, Dumpling, Puff, and Spud
      McDonald's 1992, $2-5 each.
Limited distribution. Also distributed by Avon, Wal-Mart, and Wendy's.
Markings: "©1987 Hasbro Made in China"

McDonald's

McDonald's
Row 1: Raggedy Ann & Andy-4 per set & U-3:
○ Toy 1: Raggedy Andy with Slide
○ Toy 2: Raggedy Ann with Swing
Row 2:
○ Toy 3: The Camel with the Wrinkled Knees & a Seesaw
○ Toy 4: Grouchy Bear with Carousel
○ Toy 5: U-3 The Camel
McDonald's 1989, $4-5 each.
Limited distribution.
Markings: "©1988 MacMillian Inc China"
Row 3: Rescuers Down Under-4 per set & U-3:
○ Toy 1: Jake
○ Toy 2: Cody
○ Toy 3: Wilbur
○ Toy 4: Bernard & Bianca
○ Toy 5: U-3 Bernard
McDonald's 1990, $1-2 each.
Viewers.
Markings: "©Disney China"
Row 4: Runaway Robots-6 per set:
○ Toy 1: Beck
○ Toy 2: Flame
○ Toy 3: Jab
○ Toy 4: Bolt
○ Toy 5: Coil
○ Toy 6: Skull
McDonald's 1985, $3-5 each.
Limited distribution. Also distributed by Subway (Cy*Treds).
Markings: "©85 S Colburn Made in China"
Row 4: Sea World of Ohio-3 per set:
○ Toy 7: Shamu
○ Toy 8: Dolly Dolphin
○ Also: Penny Penguin
McDonald's 1988, $5-7 each.
Limited distribution.
Markings: "©1987 Sea World Inc Made in China"

McDonald's

McDonald's

Row 1: Snow White-8 per set & U-3:
- Toy 1: Snow White & Wishing Well
- Toy 2: Happy & Grumpy
- Toy 3: Doc
- Toy 4: Dopey & Sneezy-also U-3

Row 2:
- Toy 5: Double Trouble Queen/Witch
- Toy 6: Bashful
- Toy 7: Sleepy—not shown
- Toy 8: Prince & Horse-with & without base

McDonald's 1993, $1-3 each; with base, $5.
The Prince's Horse came with and without (limited distribution) a grass base.
Markings: "©Disney China"

Row 3: Sonic The Hedgehog 3-4 per set & U-3:
- Toy 1: Sonic The Hedgehog
- Toy 2: Miles Tails Prowler-recalled
- Toy 3: Dr Ivo Robotnik
- Toy 4: Knuckles
- Toy 5: U-3 Ball

McDonald's 1994, $1-2 each; U-3, $3.
A TV cartoon series and a Sega Video Game.
Markings: "™ & ©1993 Sega China"

Row 4: Sports Balls-4 per set:
- Toy 1: Basketball
- Toy 2: Baseball
- Toys 3 & 4: Football-two colors
- Toy 5: Soccer Ball

McDonald's 1990, $3-5 each.
Limited distribution.
Tag: "©1989 McDonald's Corporation"

McDonald's

McDonald's

Row 1: Stomper Mini 4x4-8 per set & 4 U-3s:
○ Toy 1: AMC Eagle-also black with gold
○ Toy 2: Chevy S-10 also black with silver
○ Toy 3: Chevy Van-also yellow with orange
○ Toy 4: Chevy Blazer-also yellow with green
○ Toy 5: Dodge Rampage-also white with blue
○ Toy 6: Ford Ranger-also orange with yellow
Row 2:
○ Toy 7: Jeep Renegade-also orange with yellow
○ Toy 8: Toyota Tercel-also blue with yellow
○ Toy 9: U-3 Blazer
○ Toy 10: U-3 Tercel
○ Toy 11: U-3 Chevy Van
○ Toy 12: U-3 Jeep Renegade
McDonald's 1986, $2-4 each. Limited distribution.
Markings: "Stomper® Patent Pending Schaper Mfg Co Minneapolis Mn"

Row 3: Super Heroes-4 per set & U-3:
○ Toy 1: Daffy Duck as Bat-Duck
○ Toy 2: Tazmanian Devil as Taz-Flash
○ Toy 3: Petunia Pig as Wonder Pig
○ Toy 4: Bugs Bunny as Super Bugs
○ Toy 5: U-3 Daffy in Bat-Duckmobile
McDonald's 1992, $2-3 each.
Warner Brothers cartoon characters.
Markings: "™ & ©91 WBI China"
Row 3: Super Mario Brothers-4 per set & U-3:
○ Toy 1: Mario
○ Toy 2: Luigi
○ Toy 3: Goomba
○ Toy 4: Koopa Paratroopa
○ Toy 5: U-3 Mario-finger puppet
McDonald's 1991, $2-4 each.
A video game.
Markings: "©1989 Nintendo of America Inc China"

McDonald's

McDonald's
Row 1: Spiderman-8 per set:
○ Toy 1: Spiderman
○ Toy 2: Mary Jane Watson & 2 Outfits-3 pieces
○ Toy 3: Steve Parker
Row 2:
○ Toy 4: Scorpion Stingstriker
○ Toy 5: Hobgobbin Landglider
○ Toy 6: Venom Transport
○ Toy 7: Spidermobile
○ Also: Dr Octopus
McDonald's 1995, $3-5.
Markings: "©1995 Marvel China Chine"

McDonald's
Row 1: Tailspin-4 per set & 2 U-3s:
○ Toy 1: Wildcat's Flying Machine
○ Toy 2: Baloo's Sea Plane
○ Toy 3: Kit's Racing Plane
○ Toy 4: Molly's Biplane
○ Toy 5: U-3 Baloo
○ Toy 6: U-3 Wildcat
McDonald's 1990, $1-2 each; U-3s, 4-5 each.
A Disney TV cartoon series. Metal airplanes.
Markings: "©Disney China"
Row 2: Tinosaurs-8 per set:
○ Toy 1: Kobby
○ Toy 2: Link
○ Toy 3: Fern
○ Toy 4: Spell
○ Toy 5: Dinah
○ Toy 6: Tiny
○ Toy 7: Jad
○ Toy 8: Bones
McDonald's 1985, $5-7 each.
Limited distribution.
Markings: "©85 Aviva Ent Inc Tinosaurs McDonald's® Made in China"
Row 3: Tiny Toons-8 per set & U-3:
○ Toy 1: Buster Bunny
○ Toy 2: Elmyra
○ Toy 3: Dizzy Devil
○ Toy 4: Montana Max
○ Toy 5: Plucky Duck
○ Toy 6: Babs Bunny
○ Toy 7: GoGo DoDo
○ Toy 8: Sweetie-also U-3

McDonald's 1993, $1-2 each.
A Warner Brothers TV cartoon series.
Markings: "™ & ©Warner China"
Row 4: Tiny Toons Flip Cars-4 per set & 2 U-3s:
○ Toy 1: Montana Max/GoGo DoDo
○ Toy 2: Hampton/Dizzy Devil
○ Toy 3: Elmyra/Buster Bunny
○ Toy 4: Babs Bunny/Plucky Duck
○ Toy 5: U-3 GoGo DoDo
○ Toy 6: U-3 Plucky Duck
McDonald's 1990, $1-2 each; U-3s, $5-10 each.
Markings: "©1990 Warner Brothers ©1990 McDonald's Corp"

83

McDonald's

McDonald's
Row 1: Tom & Jerry Band-4 per set & U-3:
○ Toy 1: Droopy with Microphone
○ Toy 2: Tom with Keyboard
○ Toy 3: Jerry with Drums
○ Toy 4: Spike with Base
○ Toy 5: U-3 Droopy
McDonald's 1989, $5-8 each.
Limited distribution.
Markings: "©1988 Turner Entertainment Co Made in China"
Row 2: Tonka 92-5 per set & U-3:
○ Toy 1: Backhoe
○ Toy 2: Cement Mixer
○ Toy 3: Fire Truck
○ Toy 4: Loader
○ Toy 5: Dump Truck
○ Toy 6: U-3 Dump Truck
McDonald's 1992, $1-2 each; U-3, $5.
Markings: "©1992 Tonka Corp China"

Row 3: Tonka 94-4 per set & U-3:
○ Toy 1: Loader
○ Toy 2: Grader
○ Toy 3: Crane
○ Toy 4: Bulldozer
○ Toy 5: U-3 Dump Truck
McDonald's 1994, $1-2 each; U-3, $3-5.
Markings: "©1992 Tonka Corp China"
Row 4: Totally Toy Holiday-Boys-4 per set & U-3:
○ Toy 1: Mighty Max
○ Toy 2: Tattoo Machine
○ Toy 3: Key Force Truck
○ Toy 4: Attack Pack
○ Toy 5: U-3 Key Force Car
McDonald's 1993, $1-2 each.
Markings: "Hot Wheels® ©1993 Mattel Inc China"

McDonald's

McDonald's
Row 1: Totally Toy Holiday-Girls-4 per set:
○ Toy 1: Polly Pocket
○ Toys 2 & 3: Sally Secrets-shoes are hole punch
○ Toy 4: Li'l Miss Candy Stripes
○ Toys 5 & 6: Magic Nursery-also U-3
McDonald's 1993, $1-2 each; #6, $3-5.
Markings: "Made for McDonald's ©1993 Bluebird Toys China"
Row 2: Wild Friends-4 per set & U-3:
○ Toy 1: Panda
○ Toy 2: Alligator
○ Toy 3: Elephant
○ Toy 4: Gorilla
○ Toy 5: U-3 Panda
McDonald's 1992, $4-5 each; U-3, $5-8.
Limited distribution, PVC with book attached to base.
Markings: "©1992 SMI China"
Row 3: Yo, Yogi-4 per set:
○ Toy 1: Cindy (Fr-*Cindy*)
○ Toy 2: Boo Boo (Fr-*Bou-Bou*)
○ Toy 3: Huckleberry Hound (Fr-*Roquet Belles Oreilles*)
○ Toy 4: Yogi (Fr-*Yogi*)
McDonald's 1991, $5-8 each.
Limited distribution in USA & distribution in Canada.
Markings: "©1991 H-B Prod Inc China"
Row 4: Young Astronauts 92:
○ Toy 1: U-3 Ronald
McDonald's 1992, $2-3 each.
Single figurine, the regular premiums are paper puzzles.
Markings: "©1991 McDonald's Corp Young Astronauts Council™ China"
Row 4: Young Astronauts 94-4 per set & 2 U-3s:
○ Toy 2: Apollo Module
○ Toy 3: Cirrus VTOL
○ Toy 4: Space Shuttle
○ Toy 5: U-3 Fry Guy Friendly Flyer
○ Toy 6: U-3 Grimace Smiling Shuttle
○ Also: Argo Land Shuttle
McDonald's 1986, $7-9 each.
Limited distribution.
Markings: "©1986 McDonald's"

Nathan's

Nathan's
Row 1: Franksters 92-3 per set:
○ Toy 1: Rollerblades
○ Toy 2: Skateboard
○ Toy 3: Ice Skates
Nathan's Famous Hot Dogs 1992, $5-7 each. About 5-6" tall.
Markings: "Since 1916 Nathan's® (logo) ©1992 Nathan's Famous Inc Made in China"
Row 1: Franksters 93-3 per set:
○ Toy 4: Baseball
○ Toy 5: Surfer
○ Also: Swimmer
Nathan's Famous Hot Dogs 1993, $5-7 each. About 5-6" tall.
Markings: "Since 1916 Nathan's® (logo) ©1993 Nathan's Famous Inc Made in China"
Row 2: Franksters 94-4 per set:
○ Toy 1: Football
○ Toy 2: Cheerleader
○ Toy 3: Basketball
○ Toy 4: Hockey
Nathan's Famous Hot Dogs 1994, $5-7 each. About 5-6" tall.
Markings: "Since 1916 Nathan's® (logo) ©1994 Nathan's Famous Inc Made in China"

Pizza Hut

Pizza Hut & Popeye's

Row 1: Air Garfield:
◯ Toy 1: Air Garfield
Pizza Hut 1993, $1.
This figurine was inside a spaceball or attached to a parachute which is usually how he is found if not MIP.
Markings: "©1978 United Features Syndicate Inc Made in China"

Row 1: Aliens-4 per set:
◯ Toy 2: Smiley
◯ Toy 3: Little Green Man from Mars
◯ Toy 4: Space Kat
◯ Toy 5: Moon Man
Pizza Hut 1980s with logo, $10-15 each; no logos, $7-10 each.
These creatures were so popular that they were recast with the markings removed.
Markings: "Pizza Hut (logo) Made in China"

Row 2: Marsupilami Houba-Douba-3 per set:
◯ Toy 1: Jump Rope
◯ Toy 2: Glow Ball
◯ Toy 3: Yo-Yo
Pizza Hut 1994, $3-5 each.
Markings: "©Disney China"

Row 3: Pizza Box
◯ Toy 1: Pizza Box
Pizza Hut 1994, $1-2.
Inside of lid has pizza topping food molds, base is pizza crust mold, came with peel-off stickers.
No Markings

Row 3: Young Indiana Jones Chronicles-3 per set:
◯ Toy 1: Magnifying Glass
◯ Toy 2: Compass
◯ Toy 3: Telescope
Pizza Hut 1994, $2-3 each.
A TV series.
Markings: "Don't look into sun China"

Row 4: Popeye-5 per set:
◯ Toy 1: Popeye
◯ Toy 2: Olive Oyl
◯ Toy 3: Sweet Pea
◯ Toy 4: Brutus
◯ Also: Wimpy
Popeye's Famous Fried Chicken 1980 to 1994, $1 each.
About 2" tall each, came in five different colors.
Markings: "1980 KFS"

Row 4: Popeye Pencil Toppers-5 per set:
◯ Toy 5: Sweet Pea
◯ Also: Olive Oyl, Popeye, Wimpy, and Brutus
Popeye's Famous Fried Chicken 1980 to 1994.
About 1.25" tall pencil toppers.
Markings: "©1980 KFS"

Roy Rogers

Roy Rogers
Rows 1 & 2: Batting Helmets-28 teams per set:
Roy Rogers 1992, $1 each.
Markings: "Leich (logo)"
Row 3: Fun Flyers-4 per set:
○ Toy 1: Passenger Plane
○ Toy 2: Helicopter
○ Also: Jet Fighter and Jet Passenger
Roy Rogers 1989, $5-7 each.
Each came in different colors with peel-off stickers.

Markings: "Vikingplast Sweden Art NR"
Row 4: Gator Tales-4 per set:
○ Toy 1: Av Gator
○ Toy 2: Flora Gator
○ Toy 3: Investi-Gator
○ Toy 4: Skater Gator
Roy Rogers 1989, $5-7 each.
Two pieces each: the hair/hats/glasses are easy to lose.
Markings: "Mfg by Procorp Inc Made in China"

Roy Rogers
Row 1: X-Men
○ Toy 1: Cyclops vs Commando
○ Toy 2: The Blob vs Wolverine
Row 2:
○ Toy 1: Phantasia vs Storm
○ Toy 2: Rogue vs Avalanche
Roy Rogers 1995, $3-5 each.
Three pieces each, the four platforms or ground pieces fit together to form one battleground. Also distributed by Hardee's.
Markings: "™ & ©1995 Marvel"

Roy Rogers

Row 1: Skateboard Gang Kids-4 per set:
Toys 1-4: No names
Roy Rogers 1989, $4-6 each.
Two pieces each.
Markings: "Mattel Inc 1989 Made in China"
Rows 2 & 3: Snorks:
Toys 1-16: Snorks
Names: Leader-"Allstar," Girlfriend-"Casey,"
Friends: "Dimmy" & "Tooter"
Roy Rogers 1988, $3-5 each.

Over thirty different Snorks were given out! Snorks were a TV cartoon series by Hanna-Barbera, created by Fred Monnickendam for comic book characters in Belgium and Europe.
Markings: "©SEPP 1982 Wallace Berrie Schleich Hong Kong"
Row 4: Treasure Trolls-6 per set:
○ Toys 1-6: Treasure Trolls
Roy Rogers 1993, $1 each.
Also distributed by Hardee's, Long John Silvers, Sonic, and Wal-Mart.
Markings: "China"

Show Biz Pizza

Showbiz Pizza
Row 1: Chuck E Cheese-8 per set:
○ Toy 1: Chuck E Cheese
○ Toy 2: Jumpin' Chuck E Cheese
○ Toy 3: Pen Topper
○ Toy 4: Car
○ Toy 5: Van
○ Toy 6: Water Ball
○ Toy 7: Hackeysack Ball
○ Also: Jeep
Showbiz Pizza 1988-1993, $4-5 each.
The whole restaurant is for kids! The prizes are won by collecting tickets from games in the restaurant. New items are added and depleted continually. Hackeysack balls also distributed by Discovery Zone and Subway.
Markings: "©1988 Showbiz Pizza Time Inc Made in China
Row 2: Chuck E Cheese Prizes
○ Toy 1: 7" Disk
○ Toy 2: Yo-Yo's
○ Toy 3: Telescope
○ Toy 4: Watch Game
Row 3:
○ Toy 5: Stencils
○ Toy 6: Picture Super Ball
○ Toy 7: Games
○ Toy 8: Color Cup
Showbiz Pizza 1986-1993, $1-5 each.
Markings: "©1986 Showbiz Pizza Time Inc Made in China

Show Biz Pizza

Showbiz Pizza
Row 1: Chuck E Cheese Prizes:
Toys 1-4: Fluorescent Chucky
Toy 5: Parachute Chucky
Toy 6: Mini Disks-3.5" diameter
Toy 7: Blue Ribbon
Row 2:
Toy 8: Coin Holder for Quarters/Tokens
Toy 9: Comb
Toy 10: Purse
Toy 11: Pencil Case-encased water & glitter
Toy 12: Viewer
Showbiz Pizza 1986-1994, $1-2 each.
Markings: "©1988 Showbiz Pizza Time Inc Made in China"
Row 3: Chuck E Cheese Sports-3 per set:
Toy 1: Basketball
Toy 2: Baseball
Toy 3: Football

Showbiz Pizza 1990-1994, $3-5 each.
Markings: "Made in Hong Kong Showbiz Pizza Time Inc™"
Row 3: Pizza Time Theater-2 per set:
○ Toy 4: Munch
○ Toy 5: Jasper
Showbiz Pizza 1983-1993, $3-5 each.
Pizza Time Theater, Showbiz Pizza, and Chuck E Cheese refer to the same restaurant.
Markings: "©1983 Pizza Time Theater Made in Hong Kong"
Row 3: Pizza Time Theater-2 per set:
○ Toy 6: Chuck E Cheese
○ Toy 7: Helen
Showbiz Pizza 1994, $2-4 each.
These are the new images; the other PVCs are not longer available from the restaurants.
Markings: "©Showbiz Pizza Time Inc 1994 DFI China"

Sonic

Sonic

Row 1: Adventures of the Super Sonic Kids- 4 per set:
○ Toy 1: Steve
○ Also: Brin, Corkey, and Rick
Sonic 1989, $3-5 each.
Markings: "China"
Printed: "Sonic" on shirt back
Row 1: Airtoads-6 per set:
○ Toys 2-7: Airtoads-no names
Sonic 1995, $3-4 each.
On suction cups.
No Markings, Printed: "Sonic® Airtoads"
Row 2: Animal Squirters-8 per set:
○ Toy 1: Bear
○ Toy 2: Rabbit
○ Toy 3: Panda
○ Toy 4: Monkey
○ Toy 5: Hound Dog
○ Toy 6: Cat

Row 3:
○ Toy 1: Puppy
○ Toy 2: Bulldog
Sonic 1995, $1-3 each.
Ball squirters.
No Markings
Row 3: Bag-A-Wag-4 per set:
○ Toy 3: Car
○ Toy 4: Walking
○ Toy 5: Skating
○ Toy 6: Resting
Sonic 1992, $2-4 each.
Markings: "©Sonic Ind 1992 Made in China"
Row 4: Brown Bag Bowlers-4 per set:
○ Toy 1: Yellow Ball
○ Toy 2: Red Ball
○ Toy 3: Blue Ball
○ Toy 4: Orange Ball
Sonic 1994, $3-4 each.
Markings: "©1994 Sonic Industries China"

Sonic

Row 1: Brown Bag Juniors-4 per set:
Toy 1: Marbles
Toy 2: Basketball
Toy 3: Reading
Toy 4: "The Fonz"
Sonic 1989, $3-4 each.
Markings: "©Sonic Ind Made in China"
Row 2: Brown Bag Sports Buddies-4 per set:
Toy 1: Innertube Float
Toy 2: Surfboard.
Toy 3: Sled
Toy 4: Skiing
Sonic 1993, $2-4 each.
Markings: "©Sonic Ind 1993 Made in China"
Row 2: Custom Cruisers-4 per set:
Toy 5: '59 Cadillac Convertible
Also: '49 Mercury, '55 Chevy Nomad Wagon, and '57 Chevy Convertible
Sonic 1993, $4-6 each.
Markings: "©1993 Sonic Inc China"
Row 3: Dino Hops-4 per set:
○ Toy 1: Dino with Drink
○ Toy 2: Dino with Hamburger
○ Toy 3: Dino with Hot Dog
○ Toy 4: Dino with Fries
Sonic 1994, $2-4 each.
On Springs.
Markings: "©Sonic Inc 1994 China"
Row 4: Dino Squirters-4 per set:
○ Toys 1-4: No names
Sonic 1994, $1-3 each.
Squirters.
Markings: "Sonic® (logo) ©Sonic Ind Inc 1994 ©NPI 1991"

Sonic

Sonic

Row 1: Flying Food-4 per set:
○ Toy 1: Onion Ring Squadron
○ Toy 2: Melvin Mini Burger
○ Toy 3: Clyde Corn Dog
○ Toy 4: Taterites
Sonic 1994, $1-3 each.
Suction disks.
No Markings, Label: "©1994 Sonic Industries Inc Made in China"
Row 2: Glass Hangers-9 per set:
○ Toy 1: Frog
○ Toy 2: Lion
○ Toy 3: Turtle
○ Toy 4: Pig
○ Toy 5: Elephant
○ Toy 6: Beaver
○ Toy 7: Gator
○ Toy 8: Bear
○ Toy 9: Bird
Sonic 1993, $1 each.
Various colors each, to hang on the rim of a glass or vase. Also distributed by Wendy's.
No Markings
Row 3: Hair Dudes-4 per set:
○ Toys 1-4 No names
Sonic 1993, $2-4 each.
This critter came with grass seeds to grow "hair."
Markings: "©1993 Peterson-Kennedy All Rights Reserved China"
Row 4: Holiday Express-4 per set:
○ Toy 1: Engine
○ Toy 2: Hopper
○ Toy 3: Gondola
○ Toy 4: Caboose
Sonic 1993, $5-6 each.
Similar to trains distributed by Dairy Queen and White Castle.
Markings: "Made in China"
Decals: "Sonic" and "Dr Pepper"

Sonic

Row 1: Sidewalk Surfers-4 per set:
Toy 1: Mr Big Fun
Toy 2: Ms Sidewalk Savvy
Toy 3: The Mean Sidewalk Machine
Toy 4: The Sidewalk Snoot
Sonic 1989, $2-4 each.
Photo does not show cute faces (sorry).
Markings: "Sonic® (logo) Sidewalk Surfers! Made in China Sonic Industries Inc 1989."
Row 2: Sonic Fast Food Squirters-4 per set:
Toy 1: Hamburger
Toy 2: Fries
Toy 3: Drink
Toy 4: Peppermint
Sonic 1993, $2-3 each.
Water squirters.
Markings: "©1993 Sonic China"
Row 3: Sonic Kid Squirters-3 per set:
Toys 1-3: No names
Sonic 1993, $2-3 each.
Water squirters.
Markings: "Sonic® (logo) ©Sonic Ind Inc 1993 ©Namkung 1993 China"
Row 4: Super Sonic Turbo Racers-4 per set:
Toys 1-4: no names
Sonic 1993, $3-4 each.
Fluorescent.
No Markings, Sticker: "Made in China"

Sonic

Row 1: Stunt Grip Geckos-4 per set:
◯ Toy 1: Purple
◯ Toy 2: Turquoise
◯ Also: Green and Blue
Sonic 1992, $1-3 each.
Same gecko with suction cups on feet.
No Markings
Row 2: Treasure Trolls-4 per set:
◯ Toys 1-4: Treasure Trolls
Sonic 1993, $1 each.
Also distributed by Hardee's, Long John Silvers, Roy Rogers, and Wal-Mart.
Markings: "China"
Rows 3 & 4: Wacky Sackers-6 per set:
◯ Toys 1-6 Wacky Sackers-No names
Sonic 1994, $2-3 each.
Four colors each: pink, blue, green, and tan-twenty-four total.
Markings: "©1994 Sonic Industries China"

Subway

Row 1: Captain Planet-5 per set:
○ Toy 1: Earth (Quami's Ring)
○ Toy 2: Wind (Linka's Ring)
○ Toy 3: Fire (Wheeler's Ring)
○ Toy 4: Water (Gee's Ring)
○ Toy 5: Heart (Mati's Ring)
Subway 1993, $3-5 each.
Heat the blue circle with your finger to see the symbol. These rings are essential to the characters. A TV cartoon series. About 1.5" diameter.
Markings: "Subway® Made in USA ©1993 TBS & DIC UGI"
Row 2: Coneheads Pencil Toppers-4 per set:
○ Toy 1: Beldar
○ Toy 2: Marlax
○ Toy 3: Prymaat
○ Also: Connie
Subway 1993, $3-5 each.
Motion picture. About 2.25" tall.
Markings: "©1993 Paramount Pictures Made in China"
Row 3: Cy*Treds-6 per set:
○ Toy 1: Beck
○ Toy 2: Flame
○ Toy 3: Jab
○ Toy 4: Bolt
○ Toy 5: Coil
○ Toy 6: Skull
Subway 1995, $2-4 each.
Also distributed by McDonald's ("Runaway Robots"- note different markings).
Markings: "Subway® JGI & DAI China"
Row 4: Doodletop Jr-4 per set:
○ Toys: 1-4
Subway 1994, $1 each.
Spinning top markers about 2" diameter.
Markings: "Doodletop Jr Pat Pend Made in USA"
Row 4: Hackeysack Balls-5 per set:
○ Toy 5: Tilly Tomato
○ Toy 6: Pearl Onion
○ Also: Pappy Pepper, Petey Pickle, and Lenny Lettuce
Subway 1991, $1-2 each.
Reverse side shows picture of "vegetable people." Hackeysack balls also distributed by Discovery Zone and Showbiz Pizza.
Label: "Subway (logo) Made in China ©1991 Doctor's Associates Inc"

Subway

Subway
Row 1: Explore Space
○ Toy 1: Astronaut
○ Toy 2: Space Station
○ Toy 3: Space Shuttle
○ Toy 4: Lunar Lander
Subway 1994, $3-5 each.
There are variations in paint & decals.
Markings: "Subway ©1994 JGI & DAI Made in China"
Row 2: Hurricanes-4 per set:
○ Toy 1: Amanda
○ Toy 2: Cal
○ Toy 3: Gaston
○ Toy 4: Napper
Subway 1994, $3-4 each.
A TV cartoon series.
Markings: "©1994 JGI & DAI"

Row 3: Inspector Gadget-4 per set:
○ Toy 1: Surprise Squirter
○ Toy 2: Hidden Squirter
○ Toy 3: Stamp Pad-Stamp of Gadget's Face
○ Toy 4: Magnifying Glass
Subway 1994, $2-4 each.
A TV cartoon series.
Markings: "Subway ©1994 JGI & DAI ©1994 DIC Ent LP Made in China"
Row 4: Land of the Lost-4 per set:
○ Toy 1: Dimetrodon
○ Toy 2: Triceratops
○ Toy 3: Stegosaurus
○ Toy 4: Tyrannosaurus Rex
Subway 1993, $1-3 each.
From a TV series, colors may vary.
Markings: "Made in China ACE"

Subway

Row 1: Monkey Trouble-4 per set:
○ Toy 1: Eva
○ Toy 2: Eva & Dodger
○ Toy 3: Dodger
○ Toy 4: Shorty
Subway 1994, $3-4 each.
A motion picture.
Markings: "©1994 JGI DAI NLP Inc Subway® Made in China"

Row 2: Tall Tale-4 per set & U-3:
○ Toy 1: Daniel Hackett
○ Toy 2: John Henry
○ Toy 3: Pecos Bill
○ Toy 4: Paul Bunyan
○ Toy 5: U-3 Paul Bunyan on Babe The Blue Ox
Subway 1995, $3-5 each.
A Disney cartoon motion picture.
Markings: "©Disney Prod for Subway by JGI China"

Row 3: The Santa Clause-4 per set-U-3:
○ Toy 1: Santa 3-D Puzzle-3 pieces
○ Toy 2: ELFS Action Figure
○ Toy 3: Action Snow Globe-twist puzzle
○ Toy 4: U-3 Comet
○ Also: Santa Clause Action Figure
Subway 1994, $3-4 each.
A motion picture.
Markings: "Subway ©94 JGI & DAI ©94 Disney"

Row 4: Tom & Jerry-4 per set:
○ Toy 1: Skateboard Tom
○ Toy 2: Beach Buggy Jerry
○ Toy 3: Beach Buggy Tom
○ Toy 4: Skateboard Jerry
Subway 1994, $2-4 each.
About 2.25" tall.
Markings: "Subway ©1994 TEC Inc ©1994 JGI & DAI"

Taco Bell

Taco Bell
Row 1: Congo the Movie Watches-3 per set:
○ Toy 1-3: Congo the Movie Watches
Taco Bell 1995, $4-5 each.
Watches.
Markings: "™ & ©1995 Par Pic Made in China"
Row 2: Mutant Jungle Mix-Ups-6 per set:
○ Toy 1: Red Gorilla & Turquoise Elephant
○ Toy 2: Pink Elephant & Green Rhinoceros
Row 3:
○ Toy 3: Purple Rhinoceros & Turquoise Lion
○ Toy 4: Blue Lion & Violet Wart Hog
Row 4:
○ Toy 5: Orange Wart Hog & Yellow Green Crocodile
○ Toy 6: Blue Crocodile & Yellow Gorilla
Taco Bell 1995, $3-5 each.
Two animals per package-two different colors of each animal per set (only six different animals per set-twelve total). Congo the Movie. *Markings:* "Applause PWT"

Target Markets

Subway & Taco Bell & Target Markets
Row 1: Wildlife Rangers-Guard the Animals-4 per set:
○ Toy 1: Stephan, The Snow Leopard
○ Toy 2: Herman, The Polar Bear
○ Toy 3: Dan, The Lowland Gorilla
○ Toy 4: Spot, The Crevy's Zebra
Subway 1993, $2-4 each.
Markings: "Made in China"
Row 2: Busy World of Richard Scarry-2 per set:
○ Toy 1: Lowly Worm™
○ Toy 2: Heckle Cat™
Taco Bell 1993, $3-8 each.
Finger Puppets-recalled.
Markings: "©1993 Scarry CDM China"
Row 2: Honey, I Blew Up the Kid-1 item:
○ Toy 3: Honey, I Blew Up the Kid Disk
Taco Bell 1992, $3-4 each.
A motion picture.
Markings: "©Disney"
Row 2: Rocky & Bullwinkle Stampers-2 per set:
○ Toy 4: Bullwinkle-"WOSSAMOTTA U"
○ Toy 5: Rocky-"HOKEY SMOKE!"
Taco Bell 1993, $3-7 each.
Stampers.

No Markings
Row 3: Adventure Team Window Walker Figurines-4 per set:
○ Toy 1: Bungee Bob
○ Toy 2: Freefallin' Freddie
○ Toy 3: Rock Climbin' Rochelle
○ Toy 4: Tumblin' Tommy
Target Markets 1994, $2-3 each.
Markings: "Patented Made in China"
Row 4: Muppet Twisters-3 per set:
○ Toys 1-3: Same muppets, different color blocks
Target Markets 1994, $1-3 each.
Label: "©Henson 1993 Food Avenue® 1993 Target Stores® a Division of the Dayton Hudson Corporation CDM China"
Row 4: Playful Pets-3 per set:
○ Toy 4: Martinique the Bichon Puppy
○ Toy 5: Fluffy the Kitten
○ Toy 6: Max the Dalmatian
Target Markets 1994, $3-5 each.
Snow domes.
Markings: "Food Avenue® 1994 Target Stores® Made in China"

Target Markets

Target Markets & Wal-Mart
Row 1: Targeteers 92-4 per set:
○ Toy 1: Ashley
○ Toy 2: Buddy
○ Toy 3: Danielle
○ Toy 4: Ramon
Target Markets 1992, $3-5 each.
Legs, heads, and arms move.
Markings: "Copyright ST® (logo)"
Row 2: Targeteers 93-5 per set:
○ Toy 1: Ashley
○ Toy 2: Danielle
○ Toy 3: Mei-Ling
○ Toy 4: Ramon
○ Also: Buddy
Target Markets 1993, $3-5 each.
Girls with life-like hair and moving heads, boys with roller blades, moving legs and heads.
Markings: "Made in China"

Row 3: Targeteer's Cars-3 per set:
○ Toys 1-3: Same car, different colors, Kids not included
Target Markets 1992
Markings: "ST® (logo) Copyright Reg UK"
Row 3: Targeteer's Skateboard:
○ Toy 4: Skateboard with Buddy
○ Also: 3 other Skateboards with Kids
Target Markets 1993, $3-5 each.
No Markings on skateboards
Row 4: Christmas Ornaments-6 per set:
○ Toy 1: Santa Claus
○ Toy 2: Mrs Claus
○ Toy 3: Snowman
○ Toy 4: Toy Soldier
○ Toy 5: Elf
○ Toy 6: Bear
Wal-Mart 1993, $3-4 each.
Printed: "1993 Season's Greetings Shelcore®"

Wal-Mart

Wal-Mart
Row 1: GI Joe-4 per set:
○ Toy 1: Awestriker™ & Roadblock™
○ Toy 2: Persuader™ & Bazooka™
○ Toy 3: Mobat™ & Grunt™
○ Toy 4: Warthog™ & Wetsuit™
Wal-Mart 1993, $5-7 each.
About 1.5" tall.
Markings: "©1989 Hasbro Made in China"
Row 2: Lisa Frank-4 per set:
○ Toy 1: Hollywood Bear™
○ Toy 2: Markie™
○ Toy 3: Penguin Surfer™
○ Toy 4: Sneaker Kitties™
Wal-Mart 1993, $2-3 each.
Also sold retail.
Markings: "©LFI China"
Row 3: Lisa Frank 94-4 per set:
○ Toy 1: Dolphins
○ Toy 2: Ballerina Bunny™
○ Toy 3: Casey™
○ Toy 4: Panda Painter™
Wal-Mart 1994, $2-4 each.
Also sold retail.
Markings: "©LFI China"
Row 4: Potato Head Kids-4 per set:
○ Toy 1: Slick
○ Toy 2: Sabrina
○ Toy 3: Spike
○ Toy 4: Tulip
Wal-Mart 1993, $3-4 each.
Also distributed by Avon, Wendy's, and McDonald's.
Markings: "©1986 Hasbro Made in China"
Row 4: Trolls-4 per set:
○ Toy 5: Troll Necklace
○ Also: Troll pencil topper, ponytail holder, & magnet.
Wal-Mart 1993, $1-3 each.

Wal-Mart

Wal-Mart & Wendy's

Row 1: Shelcore Summer Squirters-6 per set:
○ Toy 1: Pelican
○ Toy 2: Alligator
○ Toy 3: Shark
○ Toy 4: Lobster
○ Toy 5: Clam
○ Toy 6: Frog
Wal-Mart 1994, $2-3 each.
Water Squirters.
Markings: "Summer 1994 ©1994 Shelcore Inc All Rights Reserved Made in China"
Row 2: Alf-6 per set:
○ Toy 1: Alf as Robin Hood
○ Toy 2: Alf as Little Red Riding Hood
○ Toy 3: Alf of Arabia
○ Toy 4: Alf as Third Little Pig
○ Toy 5: Sir Alf
○ Toy 6: Romeo Alf
Wendy's 1990, $2-3 each. A TV series.
Markings: "©1990 Alien Prod Made in China ©1990 Wendy's"

Row 3: Alien Mix-Ups-6 per set:
○ Toy 1: Crimson-oid
○ Toy 2: Yello-boid
○ Toy 3: Spotta-zoid
○ Toy 4: Lime-oid
○ Toy 5: Blu-zoid
○ Toy 6: Purpa-poid
Wendy's 1989, $2-3 each.
Two parts each.
Markings: "©Applause Inc China"
Row 4: All Dogs Go To Heaven-6 per set:
○ Toy 1: Carface
○ Toy 2: Charlie
○ Toy 3: Itchy
○ Toy 4: Ann Marie
○ Toy 5: Flo
○ Toy 6: King Gator
Wendy's 1989, $3-4 each.
A cartoon motion picture.
Markings: "™ ©1989 Goldcrest & Sullivan Bluth Ltd ©1989 Wendy's Int'l Inc China"

Wendy's

Wendy's
Row 1: Arts-5 per set & U-3:
Toy 1: Hamburger Water Colors
Toy 2: Red & Purple Frosty Pens
Toy 3: French Fry Chalk
Toy 4: Fast Food Crayons
Toy 5: Hamburger Crayon Puzzle
Toy 6: U-3 Wendy's Truck
Wendy's 1993, $1 each. #6, $2-4 each.
Markings: "Wendy's ©1993 Wendy's Int'l Inc Made in China"
Row 2: Cybercycles-5 per set:
Toys 1-5 Cybercycles
Toy 6: U-3 Cycle
Wendy's 1994, $2-4 each.
Markings: "©1994 Wendy's Int'l China"
Row 3: Definitely Dinosaurs 88-4 per set:
○ Toy 1: Apatosaurus
○ Toy 2: Anatosaurus
○ Toy 3: Triceratops
○ Toy 4: Tyrannosaurus Rex
Wendy's 1988, $3-5 each.
About 6" long.
Markings: Definitely Dinosaurs logo
Row 4: Definitely Dinosaurs 89-6 per set:
○ Toy 1: Ankylosaurus
○ Toy 2: Apatosaurus
○ Toy 3: Ceratosaurus
○ Toy 4: Parasaurolophus
○ Toy 5: Stegosaurus
○ Toy 6: Triceratops
Wendy's 1989, $2-4 each.
About 6" long.
Markings: Definitely Dinosaurs logo

Wendy's

Wendy's

Row 1: Dino Games-6 per set:
○ Toy 1: Dino Jam Pinball
○ Toy 2: Dino Puzzle-3 pieces in case
○ Toy 3: Dino Obstacle Course
○ Toy 4: Go Fish Dino Cards
○ Toy 5: Pterodactyl Egg Catch
○ Toy 6: Dino Maze
Wendy's 1992, $2-4 each.
Markings: "Wendy's® Dino Games ©1992 Wendy's Int'l Made in China"

Row 2: Endangered Animal Games-
5 per set & U-3:
○ Toy 1: Tiger Pinball
○ Toy 2: Sea Turtle Maze
○ Toy 3: Eagle Egg Catch Game
○ Toy 4: Crazy 8 Animal Cards
○ Toy 5: Mini Puzzle
○ Toy 6: U-3 Elephant Puzzle-3 pieces
Wendy's 1993, $2-4 each.
The puzzle includes animal-shaped pieces.
Markings: "©1993 Wendy's® China"

Row 3: Food Racers-5 per set:
○ Toy 1: Salad Scrambler
○ Toy 2: Single Sizzler
○ Toy 3: French Fry Rider
○ Toy 4: Potato Peeler
○ Toy 5: Frosty Flyer
○ Toy 6: Kid's Meal
Wendy's 1990, $2-3 each.
Markings: "©1990 Wendy's (logo) ©1990 Determined Prods Made in China"

Wendy's

Row 1: Glass Hangers-9 per set:
Toy 1: Lion
Toy 2: Bear
Toy 3: Gator
Toy 4: Turtle
Toy 5: Elephant
Toy 6: Beaver
Toy 7: Frog
Toy 8: Bird
Toy 9: Pig
Wendy's 1993, $1 each.
Also distributed by Sonic.
No Markings
Row 2: Glo Friends-12 per set:
Toy 1: Bashfulbug
Toy 2: Bookbug
Toy 3: Butterfly
Toy 4: Globug
Toy 5: Clutterbug
Toy 6: Cricket

Row 3:
○ Toy 7: Doodlebug
○ Toy 8: Bopbug
○ Toy 9: Grannybug
○ Toy 10: Skunkbug
○ Toy 11: Snail
○ Toy 12: Snugbug
Wendy's 1989, $2-4 each.
Finger puppets.
Markings: "©1986 Playskool Inc Made in China"
Row 4: Glo-Ahead-5 per set & U-3:
○ Toy 1: Reusable Stickers
○ Toy 2: "Heads will Roll" Pull Back Racer
○ Toy 3: Sucker
○ Toy 4: Eye Glasses
○ Toy 5: Flicker Disks Game
○ Toy 6: U-3 Finger Puppet-two sided, boy/girl
Wendy's 1993, $2-4 each.
Glow-in-the-dark.
Markings: "©1993 Wendy's Int'l Inc China"

Wendy's

Wendy's

Row 1: Gobots-5 per set & U-3:
○ Toy 1: Sky Flyer
○ Toy 2: Beamer
○ Toy 3: Pow-Wow
○ Toy 4: Odd Ball
○ Toy 5: U-3 Guide Star
○ Also: Breez-Helicopter
Wendy's 1986, $4-7 each.
Vehicles transform into robots.
Markings: "©Tonka Corp 1985 All Rights Reserved Japan"
Row 2: Good Sports-5 per set & U-3:
○ Toy 1: Pullback Fullback-4 pieces
○ Toy 2: Hockey-4 pieces
○ Toy 3: Golf Game-4 pieces
Row 3:
○ Toy 4: Basketball-6 pieces total
○ Toy 5: Bowling-6 pieces
○ Toy 6: U-3 Baseball
Wendy's 1994, $1-3 each.
Markings: "©1994 Wendy's Int'l Inc China"
Row 4: Goodstuff Gang-6 per set:
○ Toy 1: Wendy
○ Toy 2: Sweet Stuff
○ Toy 3: Lite Stuff
○ Toy 4: Cool Stuff
○ Toy 5: Hot Stuff
○ Toy 6: Overstuff'd
Wendy's 1985, $2-4 each.
Each came in a variety of solid colors.
Markings: "Wendy & The Goodstuff Gang Available exclusively at Wendy's Made in the USA™ & ©HW ©198 Wendy's Int'l Inc"
Row 4: Happy Moodie
○ Toy 7: Happy Moodie
Wendy's 1984, $5-10
Happy Moodies cast in other colors are rare.
Markings: "©1984 Kent Toys Inc Boyko USA Made in USA

Wendy's

Wendy's
Row 1: Jetson's Vehicles-6 per set:
○ Toy 1: Judy
○ Toy 2: Astro
○ Toy 3: Jane
Row 2:
○ Toy 4: George
○ Toy 5: Elroy
○ Toy 6: Mr Spacely
Wendy's 1989, $3-5 each.
TV cartoon series by Hanna-Barbera.
Markings: "©1989 Hanna-Barbera Prod Inc available only @ Wendy's® collect all 6 Strottman Int'l Inc Made in China"
Row 3: Jetson's Space Gliders-6 per set:
○ Toy 1: George
○ Toy 2: Elroy
○ Toy 3: Judy
○ Toy 4: Astro
○ Toy 5: Grunchee
○ Toy 6: Fergie
Wendy's 1990, $2-4 each.
A cartoon motion picture.
Markings: "©1990 UCS Jetsons® Property ©H-B Prod Inc Lic by Hamilton Prod Inc Applause™"
Row 4: Mighty Mouse-6 per set:
○ Toy 1: Mighty Mouse
○ Toy 2: Pearl Pureheart
○ Toy 3: The Cow
○ Toy 4: Scrappy
○ Toy 5: Petey Pate
○ Toy 6: Bat Bat
Wendy's 1989, $3-5 each.
On suction cups, Comic book series from the 1940s.
Markings: "™ ©VIACOM Made in China"

Wendy's

Wendy's

Row 1: Potato Head Kids 87-6 per set:
○ Toy 1: Rabbit Nubbins
○ Toy 2: Blue Mouse
○ Toy 3: Big Horn Ram
○ Toy 4: Sabrina Witch
Row 2:
○ Toy 5: Sir Scallop
○ Toy 6: Cavalier
Wendy's 1987, $3-5 each.
Three pieces each, interchangeable. Potato Head Kids were also distributed by Avon, McDonald's, and Wal-Mart.
Markings: "©1987 Hasbro Made in China"
Row 2: Potato Head Kids 88-6 per set:
○ Toy 7: Cap'n Kid
○ Toy 8: Fireman Sparky

Row 3:
○ Toy 9: Krispy
○ Toy 10: Nurse Sophie
○ Toy 11: Policeman Duke
○ Toy 12: Slugger
Wendy's 1988, $3-5 each.
Three pieces each, interchangeable. Potato Head Kids also distributed by Avon, McDonald's, and Wal-Mart.
Markings: "©1987 Hasbro Made in China"
Row 4: Rocket Writers-5 per set & U-3:
○ Toys 1-5 Rocket Writers
○ Toy 6: U-3 Explorer 7 Rocket
Wendy's 1992 42-3 each.
Five novelty writing pens.
Markings: "Wendy's® (logo) ©1992 Wendy's Int'l Inc Made in China"

Wendy's

endy's
ow 1: Saurus Sports Balls-4 per set:
 Toy 1: Basketballasaurus
 Toy 2: Baseballasaurus
 Toy 3: Footballasaurus
  Also: Soccerasaurus
endy's 1992, $3-5 each.
arkings: "©1986 Talking Tops Made in China"
ow 2: Speed Bumpers-5 per set & U-3:
 Toy 1: BUMP
 Toy 2: FUN
 Toy 3: "CRUSHER"-WOW
 Toy 4: FLY
 Toy 5: "WILD"-WILDTHING
○ Toy 6: U-3 "BAG IT!"-BAD
Wendy's 1992, $2-3 each.
Markings: "Wendy's® (logo) ©1992 Wendy's Int'l Inc Made in China"
Row 3: Speed Writers-6 per set:
○ Toys 1-6 Speed Writers
Wendy's 1991, $2-3 each.
Novelty pens, over 5" long.
Markings: "Wendy's® (logo) ©1991 Det Prod Made in China"
Row 4: Super Sky Carrier-6 per set:
○ Toys 1-3: Super Sky Carrier
Continued in next photo

Wendy's

Wendy's

Row 1: Super Sky Carrier-6 per set-continued from previous photo:
○ Toys 4-6: Super Sky Carrier
Wendy's 1990, $4-5 each.
Each premium can carry a Micro Machines Car (not included), each has peel-off stickers.
Markings: "™ & ©1990 Lewis Galoob Toys Inc Made in China"

Row 2: Techno Tows-4 per set & U-3:
○ Toy 1: Boat Car
○ Toy 2: Shovel Tow
○ Toy 3: 3-Wheeler
○ Toy 4: Tow Truck
○ Toy 5: U-3 Diamond Truck
Wendy's 1995, $1-3 each.
Markings: "©1995 Wendy's Int'l Inc China"

Row 3: Teddy Ruxpin-5 per set:
○ Toy 1: Teddy Ruxpin
○ Toy 2: Wooly What's It
○ Toy 3: Fob
○ Toy 4: Grubby Worm
○ Toy 5: Newton Gimmic-not flocked
Wendy's 1987, $4-6 each.
Flocked.
Markings: "©86 All"

Row 4: Too Cool for School-5 per set & U-3:
○ Toy 1: Hot Numbers Pad
○ Toy 2: Frosty Pencil Sharpener/Eraser
○ Toy 3: Pickle Pen
○ Toy 4: Pencil Pouch with Ruler
○ Toy 5: Hamburger Note Pad
○ Toy 6: U-3 Stencils
Wendy's 1992, $1 each.
Markings: "©1992 Wendy's China"

Wendy's

ndy's
w 1: Tricky Tints
Toy 1: Tricky Tints Flyer
ndy's 1992, $5
k has a 7" diameter. The color changes with sunlight
posure. Printed: "It Changes Colors"
w 1: UFO-Unbeliveably Fun Objects-
er set & U-3:
Toy 1: Satellite Sucker Ball
Toy 2: Squishy Saturn Ball
Toy 3: Glow-in-the-Dark Moon Ball
w 2:
Toy 4: Comet Ball
Toy 5: Bouncing Planet Ball
Toy 6: U-3 Glow-in-the-Dark Inflatable
Universe Ball
ndy's 1992, $3-5 each.
arkings: "©1992 Wendy's China"
w 3: Wacky Wind-Ups-6 per set:

○ Toy 1: Christmas Gift Hamburger
○ Toy 2: Biggie Fries
○ Toy 3: Miss Baked Potato
○ Toy 4: Jolly Hamburger
○ Toy 5: Chocolate Shake
○ Toy 6: Kid's Meal
Wendy's 1991, $1-2 each.
Wind-Ups.
Markings: "©1991 Wendy's Int'l Inc Made in China"
Row 4: Weird Writers-5 per set & U-3:
○ Toy 1: Hammer Head
○ Toy 2: Dizzy
○ Toy 3: Slimer
○ Toy 4: Trans-Rex Robot
○ Toy 5: Surfer
○ Toy 6: U-3 Boid
Wendy's 1993, $1-2 each.
Markers about 4" tall.
Markings: "©1993 Wendy's Int'l Inc Made in China"

Wendy's

Wendy's
Row 1: Wendy's Toys-2 per set:
○ Toy 1: Football
○ Toy 2: Mini Fun Flyer
Wendy's, $1-3 each.
These items are used as fill-ins between promotions.
Markings: "Wendy's (logo)"
Row 2: Wild Games-5 per set & U-3:
○ Toy 1: Pinball Target
○ Toy 2: Pinball Ski
○ Toy 3: Fries Catch Game
○ Toy 4: Mini Basketball
○ Toy 5: U-3 Soft Ball
○ Also: Fast Food Catch Game
Wendy's 1992, $3-5 each.
Markings: "Wendy's® Wild Games ©1991 Wendy's Int'l Inc Made in China"
Row 3: Write & Sniff-5 per set & U-3:
○ Toy 1: Fireman-Smoke scent
○ Toy 2: Cowboy-Leather scent
○ Toy 3: Beauty Queen-Roses scent
○ Toy 4: Baseball Player-Grass scent
○ Toy 5: Camper-Pine scent
○ Toys 6, 7, & 8: U-3 Stencils
Wendy's 1994, $1-2 each.
Markers with scented ink about 4" tall.
Markings: "©1994 Wendy's Int'l Inc"
Row 4: Yogi Bear & Friends-6 per set:
○ Toy 1: Snagglepuss
○ Toy 2: Cindy
○ Toy 3: Yogi
○ Toy 4: Boo-Boo
○ Toy 5: Ranger Smith
○ Toy 6: Huckleberry Hound
Wendy's 1991, $3-4 each.
Gliders.
Markings: "Available Exclusively at Wendy's ©1990 Hanna-Barbera Prod Inc Lic by Hamilton Projects Inc M by S11 Irvine Ca Made in China"

White Castle

White Castle
Row 1: Captain Planet-4 per set:
○ Toy 1: Wrist Pack with Decals
○ Toy 2: Wrist Pack with Magnifier
○ Toy 3: Wrist Pack with Mirror
○ Toy 4: Wrist Pack with Compass
White Castle 1995, $1-2 each.
Markings: "©1995 TBS Productions Inc"
Row 2: Castleburger Dudes-4 per set:
○ Toy 1: Castleburger Dude
○ Toy 2: Castle Drink Dude
○ Toy 3: Castle Fry Dudette
○ Toy 4: Castle Cheeseburger Dude
White Castle 1991, $1-3 each.
Markings: "©1991 White Castle System Inc China"
Row 3: Castleburger Dudes Sports Balls-per set:

○ Toy 1: Football-Castle Cheeseburger Dude
○ Toy 2: Baseball-Castleburger Dude
○ Toy 3: Basketball-Castle Drink Dude
○ Toy 4: Soccer-Castle Fries Dudette
White Castle 1993, $1-3 each.
Markings: "©1993 White Castle System Inc China"
Row 4: Fat Albert & The Cosby Kids-4 per set:
○ Toy 1: Fat Albert
○ Toy 2: Russell
○ Toy 3: Dumb Donald
○ Toys 4 & 5: Weird Harold-yellow & white sweaters
White Castle 1990, $8-10 each.
A TV cartoon series.
Markings: "©1990 William H Cosby Jr/Filmation Made in China WHK Enterprises Inc"

White Castle

White Castle

Row 1: Glow-in-the-Dark Monsters
○ Toy 1: Frankenstein
○ Toy 2: Mummy
○ Toy 3: Wolfman
White Castle 1992, $2-4 each.
About 4" tall.
Markings: "©White Castle 1992 China"
Row 1: Halloween Pez-3 per set:
○ Toy 4: Witch
○ Toy 5: Pumpkin
○ Toy 6: Skull
White Castle 1990, $2-4 each.
About 4" tall.
Markings: "Pez (logo) US Patent 3 942 683 Made in Australia"
Row 1: Nestle Rabbit
○ Toy 7: Nestle Rabbit Straw Slider
○ Also: Spoon, Cup, and Plush
White Castle 1990, $5-10 each.
Markings: "©1990 Nestle® China"

Row 2: Puppy in My Pocket-6 per set:
○ Toys 1-12 Puppy in My Pocket
White Castle 1995, $1-2 each.
Two per package.
Markings: "©MEG 1994"
Row 3: Push N Go Go Go-3 per set:
○ Toy 1: Bulldozer
○ Toy 2: Boat
○ Toy 3: Plane
White Castle 1991, $2-4 each.
Markings: "Tomy® (logo) ©1982 Tomy China"
Row 3: Silly Putty-3 per set:
○ Toys 4-6: No names
White Castle 1994, $1-2 each.
Markings: "Silly Putty® (logo) ©1991 B&S"
Row 4: Stik Mitts-4 per set:
○ Toys 1-4: No names
White Castle 1994, $1-2 each.
Florescent colors.
Printed: "Kid's Castle Meal (logo) White Castle"

White Castle

White Castle
Row 1: Stunt Grip Geckos-4 per set:
○ Toy 1: Turquoise
○ Toy 2: Purple
○ Also: Mauve & Blue
White Castle 1992, $2-4 each.
Same gecko in four different colors.
Markings: "©1992 White Castle System Inc China"
Row 1: Swat Kats-3 per set:
○ Toy 3: Razor
○ Toy 4: T-Bone
○ Toy 5: Callie
White Castle 1994, $1-3 each.
Two pieces each-launchers behind each Kat, a TV cartoon series.
Markings: "Swat Kats Radical Squadron™ ©1994 White Castle System Inc ©Namkung Promotions Inc 1994™ & ©1994 Hanna-Barbera Cartoons Inc"
Row 2: Tootsie Roll Express-4 per set:
○ Toy 1: Engine
○ Toy 2: Gondola
○ Toy 3: Hopper
○ Toy 4: Caboose
White Castle 1992, $4-6 each.
Similar to trains from Dairy Queen and Sonic.
Printed: "White Castle" and "Tootsie Roll Express"
Row 3: Triastic Take-Aparts-4 per set:
○ Toy 1: Mega-saur
○ Toy 2: Spine-asaur
○ Toy 3: Cool-asaur
○ Toy 4: Sora-saur
White Castle 1994, $2-4 each.
Also distributed by Carl's Jr.
Printed: "White Castle®"
Row 4: White Castle Bendy Pens-5 per set:
○ Toy 1: Woozy Wizard
○ Toy 2: Woofles
○ Toy 3: Wobbles
○ Toy 4: Willis
○ Toy 5: Wilfred
White Castle 1993, $3-5 each.
Printed: "White Castle® Castle Meal System Inc ©1992"

White Castle

White Castle

Row 1: White Castle Food Squirters-3 per set:
○ Toy 1: Castle Fry Dudette
○ Toy 2: Castleburger Dude
○ Toy 3: Castle Drink Dude
White Castle 1994, $3-5 each.
Water squirters.
Markings: "©1994 White Castle System Inc ©Namkung 1994"

Row 2: White Castle Meal Family 89-6 per set:
○ Toy 1: Princess Wilhelmina
○ Toy 2: Wendell
○ Toy 3: Sir Wincelot
○ Toy 4: Woozy Wizard
○ Toy 5: Woofles
○ Toy 6: Willis
White Castle 1989, $3-7 each.
Markings: "©1989 White Castle System Inc Made in China"

Row 3: White Castle Meal Family 92-5 per set:
○ Toy 1: Friar Wack
○ Toy 2: Wobbles & Woody
○ Toy 3: King Woolly & Queen Winnevere
○ Toy 4: Wally
○ Toy 5: Wilfred
White Castle 1992, $3-7 each.
Markings: "©White Castle System Inc 1992 Made in China"

Row 4: White Castle Meal Family Bubble Makers-4 per set:
○ Toy 1: Woozy Wizard
○ Toy 2: Princess Wilhelmina
○ Toy 3: Wendell
○ Also: Sir Wincelot
White Castle 1992, $3-7 each.
Heads unscrew to body bottles & soap bubbles.
Markings: "©White Castle Systems Inc"

White Castle

White Castle
Row 1: White Castle Super Balls-4 per set:
- Toy 1: Castleburger Dude
- Toy 2: Castle Drink Dude
- Toy 3: Castle Cheeseburger Dude
- Toy 4: Castle Fry Dudette

White Castle 1994, $1-3 each.
Super balls with characters in the center. About 1.15" diameter.
Markings: "China"
Printed: "©White Castle 1993"

Row 2: White Castle Water Balls-4 per set:
- Toy 1: Castle Fry Dudette
- Toy 2: Castle Cheeseburger Dude
- Toy 3: Castle Drink Dude
- Toy 4: Castleburger Dude

White Castle 1993, $1-3 each.
Ball & water inside plastic sphere; Showbiz Pizza also has one with Chuck E Cheese. 1.75" diameter.
Markings: "©1993 White Castle System Inc China"

Row 3: Wind-Up Castleburger Dudes-4 per set:
- Toy 1: Castle Fry Dudette
- Toy 2: Castle Cheeseburger Dude
- Toy 3: Castleburger Dude
- Toy 4: Castle Drink Dude

White Castle 1992, $1-3 each.
Wind-ups.
Markings: "©1992 White Castle System Inc China"

FOREIGN MARKET FAST FOOD TOYS

Note: Some of the foreign premiums are identical to the premiums distributed in the US. This section is limited to the premiums that are not identical to the National ones. This section should expand rapidly as more sets are imported and brought back by vacationers. Most of the foreign McDonald's sets are not named. Names were chosen according to their descriptions.

Foreign

Row 1: Aladdin-4 per set:
○ Toy 1: Aladdin & Jasmine-pull back racer
○ Toy 2: Genie in Lamp-twist to raise
○ Toy 3: Sultan Wobble
○ Toy 4: Jafar-arms & attached cloth cape raise

McDonald's Europe 1993, $5-10 each.
Markings: "©Disney China"

Row 2: Aristocats-4 per set:
○ Toy 1: Edgar the Butler on Motorbike
○ Toy 2: Berlioz, Toulouse & Marie in Sidecar-attached to Motorbike
○ Toy 3: O'Malley (short for: Abraham de Lacy Guiseppe Tracy Thomas)
○ Toy 4: Duchess

McDonald's Europe 1994, $5-10 each.
A cartoon motion picture.
Markings: "©Disney China"

Row 3: Astérix™-4 per set:
○ Toy 1: Obelisque
○ Toy 2: Dog
○ Toy 3: Dolphin
○ Toy 4: Astérix™

McDonald's Foreign 1994, $5-10 each. European cartoon character.
Markings: "©1994 GOSCÏNNY-UDERZO China"

Row 4: Attack Pack-4 per set:
○ Toys 1-4: Attack Pack

McDonald's Canada 1993, $3-5 each.
Markings: "Hot Wheels Mattel (logo)"

Foreign

Foreign

Row 1: Barbie 93-4 per set:
◯ Toy 1: Sea Holiday
◯ Toy 2: Crystal
◯ Toy 3: Hollywood Hair
◯ Toy 4: My First Ballerina
McDonald's Europe 1993, $5-10 each.
Markings: "Made for McDonald's ©1993 Mattel Inc Made in China"
Row 1: Beauty & The Beast-4 per set:
◯ Toy 5: Switch Bell
◯ Also: The Beast, Chip, & Cogsworth
McDonald's Europe 1992, $5-10 each.
Markings: "©1992 McDonald's Corp ©Disney"
Row 2: Dragonettes-4 per set:
◯ Toys 1-4: Dragonettes
McDonald's Europe 1992, $5-10 each.
Markings: "©McDonald's 1988 China"
Row 3: Euro-Disney-4 per set:
◯ Toy 1: Chip 'n' Dale in Engine
◯ Toy 2: Tigger in Tea Cup Ride
◯ Toy 3: Captain Hook in Ship
◯ Toy 4: Dalmatian in Fire Engine
McDonald's Europe, $5-10 each.
Markings: "©Disney China"
Row 3: Five Lucky Stars-5 per set:
◯ Toy 5: Precious
◯ Also: Bucks, Lucky, Happy, and Richie (all dogs)
McDonald's Orient 1994, $10 each.
Markings: "©1994 MCD Corp KY China"
Row 4: Flintstones-4 per set:
◯ Toy 1: Wilma-Town of Bedrock
◯ Toy 2: Barney-Bowling-2 pieces
◯ Toy 3: Fred-Hard Hat Area
◯ Toy 4: Dino-Bone Diner
Burger King Ltd England 1993, $10 each.
Car tops removable.
Markings: "©1993 Hanna-Barbera Prod Inc Burger King Ltd China"

Foreign

Foreign
Row 1: Flintstones the Movie-4 per set:
○ Toy 1: Wilma & Dino
○ Toy 2: Roc Donald's-with 4 sliding wall panels with peel-off stickers
○ Toy 3: Fred on Brontosaurus
○ Toy 4: Bedrock RTD-with peel-off stickers
McDonald's Europe 1994, $5-10 each.
Markings: "The Flintstones™ (logo) ©UCS & Amblin™ H-B Inc China"
Row 2: Gladiators-6 per set:
○ Toys 1-6 Gladiators
Pizza Hut Europe 1992, $10 each. Action figures, like the one shown. Each came with a combat baton.
No Markings
Row 3: Gliedertiere Floppy Puppet-4 per set:
○ Toy 1: Lion
○ Toy 2: Elephant
○ Toy 3: Dog
○ Toy 4: Donkey
McDonald's Europe, $5-10 each.
Push base down to make them "fall apart"
Markings: "CE ©McDonald's Corp Made by Kids Promotion Grafing"

Foreign

Foreign

Row 1: Les Animaux de la Jungle-6 per set:
Toy 1: Ostrich
Toy 2: Elephant
Toy 3: Hippo
Toy 4: Lion
Toy 5: Giraffe
Toy 6: Monkey
McDonald's Canada 1992, $2-3 each. Puzzles, also distributed by Chick-Fil-A.
Markings: "McDonald's"
Row 2: Lion King-4 per set:
Toy 1: Scar
Toy 2: Young Nala
Toy 3: Zazu
Toy 4: Pumbaa and Timon
McDonald's Europe 1994, $5-10 each.

Wind-Ups, Lion King also distributed by Burger King.
Markings: "©Disney China"
Row 3: Looney Tunes-4 per set:
○ Toy 1: Sylvester & Tweety Bird in Airplane
○ Toy 2: Bugs Bunny on Scooter
○ Toy 3: Daffy Duck in Car
○ Toy 4: Wile E Coyote & Road Runner on a Handcart
McDonald's Canada 1989, $5-7 each.
Markings: "Charan Ind ©Warner Brothers Inc 1989 China ©1989 McDonald's China"
Row 3: Los Muppet Bebés en sus Rapimoviles-4 per set:
○ Toy 5: Bebé Rene ("Baby Frog"-Kermit)
○ Also: Miss Piggy, Fozzie, and Gonzo
McDonald's Puerto Rico 1992, $10 each.
Markings: "MR ©1992 Henson China"

Foreign

Foreign
Row 1: McCharacters-4 per set:
○ Toy 1: Grimace
○ Also: Ronald, Birdie, and Hamburgular
McDonald's Canada 1985, $6-8 each.
Markings: "McDonald's® ®1985 Made in Canada"

Foreign
Row 1: McAirport-4 per set:
○ Toy 1: Ronald's Airplane Service Truck
○ Toy 2: Hamburgular's Airplane Service Tractor
○ Toy 3: Grimace's Jumbo Jet
○ Toy 4: Birdie's Helicopter-2 pieces
McDonald's Europe 1995, $5-10 each.
Markings: "©1995 McDonald's Corp Macau"
Row 2: McBand-4 per set:
○ Toy 1: Grimace
○ Toy 2: Ronald
○ Toy 3: Hamburgular
○ Toy 4: Birdie
McDonald's Europe 1993, $5-10
Wind-up for motion.
Markings: "©1993 McDonald's Corp China"
Row 3: McCharacters in Cars-4 per set:
○ Toy 1: Grimace-2 piece convertible
○ Also: Ronald, Birdie, and Hamburgular
McDonald's Europe 1991, $5-10 each.
Markings: "©1991 McDonald's China"
Row 3: McCharacters in Sports Vehicles-4 per set:
○ Toy 2: Grimace on Motorized Skateboard
○ Toy 3: Birdie on Motorscooter
○ Toy 4: Ronald in Racer
○ Toy 5: Hamburgular on Jet Ski
McDonald's Europe 1992, $5-10 each.
Markings: "©1992 McDonald's Corp China"
Row 4: McDonald's Akrobat-3 per set:
○ Toy 1: Hamburgular
○ Toy 2: Birdie
○ Toy 3: Ronald
McDonald's Europe, $5-10 each.
Throw them on the wall or window and the sticky feet and hands cling, allowing them to walk down the wall. Similar set distributed by Target Markets- "Adventure Team."
No Markings
Row 4: McDonald's Flyer
○ Toy 4: Ronald McDonald's Flyer
McDonald's Canada 1994, $3-4 each.
Markings: "Fabrique au Canada"

Foreign

Foreign

Row 1: McDonald's Rub & Draw Templates-per set:
 Toy 1: Ronald
 Toy 2: Hamburgular
McDonald's Europe 1993, $2-5 each.
Markings: "©1993 McDonald's Corp Simon Marketing Int eleich Made in Italy"

Row 2: McDonald's Summer Fun
 Toy 1: Bubble Maker Wand
McDonald's Europe 1992, $2-5 each.
Markings: "©1992 McDonald's Corp Simon Marketing Int ade in Italy"

Row 2: McMeal-1 unit:
 Toy 2: Tray with Placemat
 Toy 3: Shake
 Toy 4: Fries
 Toy 5: Hamburger
McDonald's Japan, $5-10
Erasers, about 2".
No Markings

Row 3: McMoon Buggies-4 per set:
 ○ Toy 1: Ronald
 ○ Toy 2: McRobot
 ○ Toy 3: Grimace
 ○ Toy 4: McSpace Shuttle
McDonald's Europe 1995, $5-10 each.
Markings: "©1995 McDonald's Corp China"

Row 4: McRockin' Fast Food-4 per set:
 ○ Toy 1: Cheeseburger
 ○ Toy 2: Fries
 ○ Toy 3: McFish
 ○ Toy 4: Drink
McDonald's Europe 1991, $5-10 each.
Wind-Ups.
Markings: "©1991 McDonald's Corp Made in China"

Foreign

Foreign
Row 1: McSpace Rev-Ups-4 per set:
○ Toy 1: Birdie
○ Toy 2: Ronald's Capsule
○ Toy 3: Fry Girl's UFO
○ Toy 4: Grimace
McDonald's Europe 1992, $5-10 each.
Markings: "©1992 McDonald's Corp China"
Row 2: McSports
○ Toy 1: Ronald on Trampoline
○ Toy 2: Birdie Plays Tennis
○ Toy 3: Grimace Plays Soccer
○ Toy 4: Hamburgular Lifts Weights
McDonald's Europe 1993, $5-10 each.
Turn the rod to make them move, connect together to make them all move together.
Markings: "©1993 McDonald's Corp China"
Row 3: McTown-4 per set:
○ Toy 1: Restaurant with Ronald
○ Toy 2: Fruit Market with Birdie
○ Toy 3: Toy Shop with Grimace
○ Toy 4: Fire Station with Fry Guys
McDonald's Europe 1993, $5-10 each.
The detail scenes are peel-off stickers.
Markings: "©1993 McDonald's Corp China"
Row 4: McTransports-4 per set:
○ Toy 1: Ronald's Diesel
○ Toy 2: Hamburgular's Bus
○ Toy 3: Birdie's Hydrofoil
○ Toy 4: Grimace's Plane
McDonald's Orient 1993, $5-10 each.
Markings: "©1993 McDonald's Corp"

Foreign

Foreign
Row 1: McWinter Sports-4 per set:
Toy 1: Grimace on Snow Tractor
Toy 2: Ronald on Skis
Toy 3: Birdie Figure Skating
Toy 4: Hamburgular in Snow Mobile Pulling Sled
McDonald's Europe 1994, $5-10 each.
Markings: "©1994 McDonald's Corp China"
Row 2: Mr Kiasu-4 per set:
Toy 1: "Everything also number one!"
Also: "Everything also I want!," "Everything also want extra!," and "Everything also must grab!"
McDonald's Japan 1993, $5-10 each.
Same character in different poses.
Markings: "©1993 McDonald's Corp China"
Row 2: Olympic McNuggets-? per set:
Toy 2: Relay Runner
McDonald's Europe 1988, $5-10 each.
Three pieces.
Markings: Arches logo
Row 3: Peanuts-4 per set:
○ Toy 1: Snoopy as the Red Baron
○ Toy 2: Lucy
○ Toy 3: Woodstock
○ Toy 4: Charlie Brown
McDonald's Canada 1989, $7-10 each.
Markings: "©1958, 1966 UFS Inc China"
Row 4: Robin Hood Rad Badges-4 per set:
○ Toy 1: Sheriff of Nottingham with Robin Hood Wanted Poster
○ Toy 2: Maid Marian & Robin Hood
○ Toy 3: Little John, Sir Hiss, & Prince John
○ Also: One other
Burger King Ltd England 1994, $10 each.
A Disney cartoon motion picture.
Markings: "©Disney Made in China"

Foreign

Foreign

Row 1: Sonic The Hedgehog Sega Zip Strips- 4 per set:
○ Toy 1: Sonic Canister
○ Toy 2: Dr Robotnik Gyroscope
○ Toy 3: Sonic Wheel
○ Toy 4: Two Tails Flyer
Burger King Ltd Europe 1993, $10 each.
Markings: "©Sega Entps Ltd 1991 ©1993 Burger King Ltd Made in China"

Row 2: Taz Mania Crazies!-4 per set:
○ Toy 1: Tree Tote Taz Carry Case-3 pieces
○ Toy 2: Fast Forward Frinzied Taz Pull Back
○ Toy 3: Tornado Spinner-3 pieces
○ Toy 4: Wild Wind-Up Wheelie Taz Cycle- 2 pieces
Burger King Ltd England 1993, $10 each.
Markings: "©1993 Warner Bros Burger King Ltd China"

Row 3: Welcome Year of the Rooster-4 per set:
○ Toy 1: Wealthy Willy
○ Toy 2: Healthy Henry
○ Toy 3: Happy Harry
○ Toy 4: Lucky Larry
McDonald's Orient 1993, $10 each.
Markings: "©1993 McDonald's Corp Made in China"

PLUSH & BIG

Note: Most, but not all, of these plush toys were sold by the restaurants, and not given away with the kid's meals. For convenience of photography, this section also includes the oversized toys. These toys are not in strict alphabetical order. If you collect these plush and big or oversized toys look for them. In general the smaller plush are listed first. Hand puppets are also included here. The name of the set is not necessarily the name of the character - an example of this are the Alf hand puppets, which are listed under the "Many Faces of Alf." Enjoy!

Plush & Big
○ Toy 1: King Burger
Burger King 1970s, $10-20.
Printed fabric, about 13-14" tall.
Printed: "Made in USA"
○ Toy 2: Ronald McDonald
McDonald's 1984, $10-20.
Printed fabric, about 12" tall.
Tag: "Ronald McDonald® ©1984 McDonald's Corp Group II"

Plush and Big

Plush & Big
Row 1: Aladdin Hidden Treasures
○ Toy 1: Abu
○ Toy 2: Iago
○ Toy 3: Jasmine & Rajah
○ Toy 4: Aladdin & Jasmine
○ Toy 5: Aladdin
Burger King 1994, $1-2 each.
Three pieces each-a box with an inflatable character inside.
Markings: "Disney" and "Burger King Kids Club"

Plush & Big
Row 1: Amazing Wildlife-8 per set:
○ Toy 1: Asiatic Lion
○ Toy 2: Chimpanzee
○ Toy 3: Koala
○ Toy 4: African Elephant
Row 2:
○ Toy 5: Dromedary Camel
○ Toy 6: Galapagos Tortoise
○ Toy 7: Polar Bear
○ Toy 8: Siberian Tiger
McDonald's 1995, $1-2 each.
About 4" tall.
Tag: "National Wildlife Federation® (logo) ©1994 McDonald's Corp"
Row 3: Cinderella-2 per set:
○ Toy 1: Gus
○ Toy 2: Jaques
McDonald's 1987, $4-10 each.
About 3" tall
Row 4: Flintstones-4 per set:
○ Toy 1: Fred & Wilma
○ Toy 2: Barney & Betty
○ Toy 3: Bamm-Bamm & Pebbles
○ Toy 4: Hoppy & Dino
Denny's 1989, $5-9 each.
Two per package, about 3-4" tall.
Tag: "©Hanna-Barbera Productions"

Plush and Big

Plush & Big

Row 1: A & W Bear
Toy 1: A & W Bear
A & W Drive-ins, $5-10.
About 13" sitting height.
Tag: "Canasia Toys and Gifts Inc Downsview Ontario"
Row 1: After Dark
Toy 2: After Dark Flyer
Burger King 1992, $3-5.
Glows-in-the-dark, 9" diameter.
Markings: "Humphery Flyer Made In USA"

Plush and Big

Plush & Big
Row 1: Beauty & The Beast-4 per set:
○ Toy 1: Beast
○ Toy 2: Belle
Row 2:
○ Toy 3: Chip
○ Toy 4: Cogsworth
Pizza Hut 1992, $3-4 each. Flexible hand puppets 5-8" tall.
Markings: "Made in China"

Plush & Big
Row 1: California Raisins III-4 per set:
○ Toy 1: "Hardee's Soft Raisin Microphone"
○ Toy 2: "Hardee's Soft Raisin Sunglasses"
Row 2:
○ Toy 3: "Hardee's Soft Raisin Female Raisin"
○ Toy 4: "Hardee's Soft Raisin Conga Dancer"
Hardee's 1989, $3-5 each. About 6" tall. These are the third Raisin premiums in the Kid's Meal.
Tag: "Applause...©1988 CALRAB...Hardee's"

Plush and Big

Plush & Big
Row 1: Alvin & The Chipmunks-3 per set:
○ Toy 1: Alvin
○ Toy 2: Simon
○ Toy 3: Theodore
Burger King 1987, $4-7 each. About 10" tall.
Tag: "©1988 Bagdasaria Productions CBS Toys A Division of CBS Inc"

Plush & Big
Row 1: Christmas Giveaways-3 per set:
○ Toy 1: Chuck E Cheese Showbiz Pizza 1988, $16-20. About 12" tall, another Chuck E is 20" tall.
Tag: "©1988 Showbiz Pizza Time Inc"
○ Toy 2: Willis
○ Also: Woofies and Wilfred White Castle 1989, $3-7 each. About 4-5" tall.
Tag: "©1989 White Castle System Inc"

Plush and Big

Plush & Big
Row 1: Chuck E Cheese
○ Toy 1: Chuck E Cheese
○ Toy 2: Jasper
○ Toy 3: Helen
Showbiz Pizza 1988, $6-7 each.
Tag: "©1988 Showbiz Pizza Time Inc"
Row 2: Chuck E Cheese Banks
○ Toy 1: Chuck E Cheese
○ Toy 2: Helen
○ Toy 3: Jasper
Showbiz Pizza 1993, $6-8 each.
PVC banks about 6" tall.
Markings: "©1993 Showbiz Pizza Time Inc China Dennis Foland Inc"

Plush & Big
Row 1: Coca-Cola Bear
Hardee's 1993, $10.
About 8" sitting.
Tag: "Coca-Cola® Brand Plush Design ©1993 The Coca-Cola Company"
○ Toy 2: Dairy Queen Bear
Dairy Queen, $5-7.
About 8" tall, has ribbon with Dairy Queen logos.
Tag: "An Animal Fair Inc® Product Minneapolis Minnesota"
Row 2: Crayola Bears-4 per set:
Burger King 1986, $5-7 each.
About 7" tall.
Tag: "©1986 Graphics International"

Plush & Big
Row 1: Casper
○ Toy 1: Casper
○ Toy 2: Stretch
○ Toy 3: Fatso
○ Toy 4: Stinkie
Pizza Hut 1995, $3-5 each. 6-9" tall, glow-in-the-dark flexible hand puppets. From the Casper motion picture.
Markings: "Casper ©1995 UCS & Amblin TM Harvey Made in China"

Plush & Big
Row 1: Eureeka's Castle-3 per set:
○ Toy 1: Eureeka
○ Toy 2: Magellan
○ Toy 3: Batly
Pizza Hut 1990, $3-5 each. Flexible hand puppets, about 4-7" tall.
Markings: "Eureeka's Castle™ ©1990 MTV Networks Made in China"
Row 2: Furskins-4 per set:
○ Toy 1: Farrell
○ Toy 2: Hattie
○ Toy 3: Dudley
○ Toy 4: Boone
Wendy's 1986, $5-8 each. About 6" tall, clothes, hats, & boots removable.
Tag: "Graphics International Inc...©1986 Original Applachian Artwork Inc"

Plush and Big

Plush & Big
Row 1: Happy Talk Sprites-4 per set:
○ Toy 1: Spark
○ Toy 2: Champ
○ Toy 3: Twink
○ Toy 4: Romeo
Taco Bell 1983, $5-7 each.
About 4" sitting, they have a motion squeaker.
Tag: "Made for Taco Bell Graphics International Inc...©1983 Hallmark Cards Inc Made in China"
Row 2: Hugga Bunch-4 per set:
○ Toy 1: Gigglet
○ Toy 2: Fluffer
○ Toy 3: Hug-A-Bye
○ Toy 4: Tuggins
Taco Bell 1984, $4-6 each.
About 7" long.
Tag: "Graphics International Inc...©1984 Hallmark Cards Inc"

Plush and Big

Plush & Big

Row 1: Halloween Surprises-4 per set:
- Toy 1: Bat in Stump
- Toy 2: Ghost in Grocery Bag
- Toy 3: Goblin in Kettle
- Toy 4: Cat in Pumpkin

Hardee's 1989, $3-5 each.
Plush figure inside a PVC container.
Tag: "Graphics Int's Inc...©1989 Hallmark Cards Inc"

Row 2: Holiday Huggables-4 per set:
- Toys 1-3 Holiday Huggables
- Also: one other

White Castle 1990, $3-5 each.
About 5" tall.
Tag: "Whitecastle® ©1990 Graphics International Inc"

Row 3: Little Caesar:
- ○ Toy 1: Little Caesar Finger Puppet

Little Caesar's Pizza 1990, $2-5 each.
About 6" tall.
Tag: "©1990 LCE Inc Little Caesars is a Trademark of LCE Inc"

Row 3: Little Mermaid-2 per set:
- ○ Toy 1: Flounder
- ○ Toy 2: Sebastian

McDonald's 1989, $2-4 each.
3-4" long.
Tag: "©The Walt Disney Company" and the Arches logo

Plush and Big

Plush & Big
Row 1: Land Before Time-6 per set:
○ Toy 1: Sharptooth
○ Toy 2: Cara
○ Toy 3: Duckie
Row 2:
○ Toy 4: Littlefoot
○ Toy 5: Spike
○ Toy 6: Petrie
Pizza Hut 1988, $3-5 each. Flexible hand puppets, 5-8" tall.
Markings: "©1988 UCS & Amblin Made in China"

Plush & Big
Row 1: The Many Faces of Alf-4 per set:
○ Toy 1: The Chef
○ Toy 2: Born to Rock Musician
Row 2:
○ Toy 3: Baseball Player
○ Toy 4: Hawaiian Tourist
Burger King 1988, $6-9 each. Hand puppets, about 11" tall.
Tag: "® ©1988 Alien Productions"

Plush and Big

Plush & Big
Row 1: Michael Jordan Fitness Fun-8 per set:
○ Toy 1: Soccer-inflatable
○ Toy 2: Baseball
○ Toy 3: Mini-Football
○ Toy 4: Mini-Basketball
Row 2:
○ Toy 5: Disk
○ Toy 6: Jump Rope
○ Toy 7: Stopwatch
○ Toy 8: Waterbottle
McDonald's 1992, $2-5 each.
Markings: "©1991 McDonald's Corp ©Jump Inc China"

Plush & Big
Row 1: Mickey's Christmas Carol-5 per set:
○ Toy 1: Mickey as Bob Cratchet
○ Toy 2: Minnie as Mrs Cratchet
○ Toy 3: Goofy as Jacob Marley
Row 2:
○ Toy 4: Donald as Scrooge's Nephew Fred
○ Toy 5: Uncle Scrooge as Ebeneezer Scrooge
Hardee's 1984, $4-5 each. About 6" sitting.
Tag: "Mickey's Christmas Carol...©Walt Disney Productions"

Plush and Big

Plush & Big
Row 1: Muppet Babies Christmas Carol-
3 per set:
○ Toy 1: Kermit
○ Toy 2: Miss Piggy
○ Toy 3: Fozzie
McDonald's 1988, $4-6 each.
About 7" sitting, clothes & hats are removable.
Tag: "©1987 Henson Associates Inc"
Row 2: Noid:
○ Toy 1: Noid
Domino's Pizza 1994, $5-7
About 10" sitting.
Row 2: Pinocchio Summer Inflatables-4 per set:
○ Toy 2: Pinochio Beach Ball
(Continued in next photo)

Plush & Big
Row 1: Pinocchio Summer Inflatables-4 per set: (continued from previous photo)
○ Toy 2: Jiminy Cricket Flyer
○ Toy 3: Monstro the Whale
○ Toy 4: Figaro Bobber
Burger King 1992, $2-3 each.
About 7-12", inflatables.
Printed: "©Disney Burger King Kid's Club (logo)"
Row 2: Pound Puppies 86-4 per set:
○ Toys 1-4: No names
Hardee's 1986, $2-4 each.
About 7-8" long.
No tags, Pound Puppies logo on sides.
Row 3: Pur-r-ries & Pound Puppies 87-5 per set:
○ Toy 1: Kitten
○ Toy 2: Kitten
○ Toy 3: Bulldog
○ Toy 4: Dalmatian
○ Toy 5: Hound Dog
Hardee's 1987, $2-5 each.
About 7-8" long. Others also sold in stores.
No tags, Pound Puppies logo on sides

Plush and Big

Plush & Big
Row 1: Purr-Tenders-4 per set:
○ Toy 1: Scamp-Purr
○ Toy 2: Hop-Purr
○ Toy 3: Romp-Purr
○ Toy 4: Flop-Purr
Hardee's 1988, $2-4 each.
About 7" tall, these are cats that are pretending to be other animals-see PVCs in Burger King section.
Tag: "Graphics International Inc...©1987 Hallmark Cards"

Row 2: Shirt Tales-5 per set:
○ Toy 1: Rick-"Wild 'n Crazy"
○ Toy 2: Bogey-"Top Banana"
○ Toy 3: Pammy-"Cuddly"
○ Toy 4: Tyg
○ Toy 5: Digger-"Hug Me"
Hardee's 1983, $4-6 each.
About 7: tall, a Hanna-Barbera TV cartoon series.
Tag: "Shirt Tales™"

Plush and Big

Plush & Big

Row 1: Mini-Plush Ronald:
◯ Toy 1: Ronald
McDonald's 1981, $3-5 each.
Printed: "©1981 McDonald's Corp"
Row 1: Oliver & Company-2 per set:
◯ Toy 2: Oliver
◯ Toy 3: Dodger
McDonald's 1988, $3-5 each.
About 3-4" tall.
Row 2: Rescuers Down Under-2 per set:
◯ Toy 1: Miss Bianca
◯ Toy 2: Bernard
McDonald's 1990, $3-5 each.
Flocked, about 3-4" tall.

Row 2: Rudolph
◯ Toy 3: Rudolph
McDonald's 1985, $4-6 each.
About 3.5" tall.
Tag: Arches logo & "Coca-Cola (logo)
Row 3: Rodney & Friends-4 per set:
◯ Toy 1: Rodney
◯ Toy 2: Rhonda
Row 4:
◯ Toy 3: Randy
◯ Toy 4: Ramona
Burger King 1985, $5-6 each.
About 5" long, Rhonda's red-dotted apron is removable
Tag: "Graphics International Inc ...©1986 Hallmark Cards Inc"

Plush and Big

Plush & Big

Row 1: Shoney Bear-2 per set:
○ Toy 1: Shoney Bear
○ Also: Shoney Bear Bank
Shoney's Restaurant 1986, $5-6 each.
Tag: "Shoney Bear"
Row 1: Chuck E Cheese
○ Toy 2: Chuck E Cheese Drink Container
Showbiz Pizza 1994, $1-3. About 10" tall.
Markings: "©1994 Showbiz Pizza Time Inc Made in Canada"
Row 2: The Simpsons-5 per set:
○ Toy 1: Homer
○ Toy 2: Marge
○ Toy 3: Bart-skateboard tag missing
○ Toy 4: Lisa
○ Toy 5: Maggie
Burger King 1990, $3-5 each. 7-12" tall. Krusty the Clown is also available from retail dealers in the same size.
Tag: "Matt Groening The Simpsons™ & ©1990 20th C Fox F C"

Plush & Big

Row 1: Tag Along
○ Toy 1: Tag Along the Tiger
Sambo's 1978, $25-30
Tag: "Made exclusively for Sambo's© ®Dakin & Co 1978 San Francisco Ca"
Row 1: Walt Disney Classics-5 per set:
○ Toy 2: Pinocchio
○ Toy 3: Dumbo
Row 2:
○ Toy 4: Bambi
○ Toy 5: Lucky
○ Toy 6: Lady (& the Tramp)
Hardee's 1985, $5-7 each. About 7" tall.
Tag: "©Walt Disney Productions"

Plush and Big

Plush & Big

Row 1: Where in The World is Carmen Sandiego?-5 per set & U-3:
- Toy 1: Secret Cup-false bottom
- Toy 2: Book/Binoculars
- Toy 3: Passport Kit
- Toy 4: Ruler/Periscope
- Toy 5: Pen/Magnifier
- Toy 6: U-3 Attache Case

Wendy's 1994, $1-3 each.
Software program and TV cartoon series.
Markings: "®Broderbund Software Inc Wendy's Int'l Inc China"

Row 2: World Wildlife Fund-4 per set:
- Toy 1: Tiger
- Toy 2: Panda
- Toy 3: Snow Leopard
- Toy 4: Koala

Wendy's 1988 45-7 each.
About 6" tall.
Tag: "World Wildlife Fund ©1988 Determined Production Inc"

INDEX

This index is designed to help find unknown pieces. The major categories are listed here. Find the character or item then check the restaurant for identification. For example: If you have a wheelbarrow: 1) find the name Wheelbarrow in this index 2) check pages 59 and page 78 to see which color you have, either a green or a brown wheelbarrow 3) check your box of toys to see if you have the associated characters-either Papa Berenstain Bear or Snoopy. Many accessories and small parts are easy to loose and get separated from the characters. Most small parts belong to McDonald's, with some from Burger King and Wendy's. Look through those sections first if you have a part you want to identify and its not found in the index.

The Restaurant names and other sections are abbreviated:
7-Eleven=7-Eleven
A=Arby's
B=Blake's Lota Burger
BB=Big Boy's
BK=Burger King
CFA=Chick-Fil-A
CJ=Carl's Jr.
D=Denny's
DD=Dunkan Donuts
DP=Dominos Pizza
DQ=Dairy Queen
DZ=Discovery Zone
F=Foreign
H=Hardee's
IHOP= International House of Pancakes
JB=Jack-in-the-Box Chicken
KFC=Kentucky Fried Chicken
KM=K-Mart
L=Lee's Famous Fried Chicken
LC= Little Caesars Pizza
LJS=Long John Silvers
M=McDonald's
N=Nathan's Hot Dogs
P=Plush & Big
PFC=Popeye's Fried Chicken
PH=Pizza Hut
RR+Roy Rogers
S=Sonic
SW=Subway
SP=Showbiz Pizza
TB=Taco Bell
TM=Target Markets
W=Wendy's
WC=White Castle
WM=Wal-Mart

Alf-**P, W,** 104, 138

Archery
  Alf-**W,** 104
  Swan Princess-**H,** 47

Archie-**BK, M,** 17, 77

Army/GI Joe
  Attack Pack-**F, M,** 55, 120
  Cabbage Patch-**M,** 60
  Christmas Ornaments-**WM,** 102
  GI Joe-**WM,** 103
  Kids Pick-Nic-**DQ,** 35

Astronauts/Space/Aliens
  Alien Mix Up-**W,** 104
  Aliens-**PH,** 87
  Astrosniks-**M,** 55
  Attack Pack-**M,** 84
  Bobby's World-**M,** 60
  Cosmic Flyers-**KM,** 51
  Dennis the Menace-**DQ,** 33
  Disneyland 40th-**M,** 62
  Explore Space-**SW,** 98
  Happy Birthday-**M,** 65
  Jetsons-**D, DQ, W,** 34, 39, 109
  McDonald's Airport-**M,** 70
  McDonald's Olympic Sports
    Badges-**M,** 73
  McMoon Buggies-**F,** 125
  McSpace-**F,** 126
  New Food Changeables-**M,** 77
  Rocket Writers-**W,** 110
  Spacebase Racers-**BK,** 28
  Space Shuttle-**DQ,** 36
  Super Sky Carrier-**W,** 111, 112
  UFO-**W,** 113
  Young Astronauts-**M,** 85
  Z-Bots-**BK,** 29

Balls-non-sports
  Barbie-**M,** 57, 58
  Bloom Ball-**DQ,** 32
  Hackeysack-**DZ, SP, SW,**
    40, 90, 97
  Jetson's Planet Balls-**D,** 39
  Little Caesar-**LC,** 52
  Marsupilami Houba-Douba
    -**PH,** 87
  Nerfuls-**BK,** 27
  Sonic, the Hedgehog-**M,** 81
  Super Balls-**SP, WC,** 90, 119
  UFO-**W,** 113
  Water Balls-**SP, WC,** 91, 119

Balls-sports-also see individual
  types of balls
  Castleburger Dudes Sports
    Balls -**WC,** 115
  Michael Jordan-**P,** 139
  Mini Sports Games-**BK,** 26
  Saurus Sports Balls-**W,** 111
  Stik Mitts-**WC,** 116

Ballerinas/Dancers
  Barbie-**M,** 57, 121
  Flintstones First 30 Years-**H,** 44
  Lisa Frank-**WM,** 103
  McDonald's Circus Parade
    -**M,** 70
  Smurf-**H,** 46

Barbie
  Barbie-**F, M,** 57, 58, 65, 121

Baseball
  Alf-**P,** 138
  Big Boy-**BB,** 16
  Baseball Helmets-**RR,** 88
  Basic 4-**M,** 58
  Burger King Kid Transporters
    -**BK,** 20
  Castleburger Dudes-**WC,** 115
  Chuck E Cheese-**SP,** 91
  Franksters-**N,** 86
  Fry Benders-**M,** 63
  Good Sports-**W,** 108
  McNugget Buddies-**M,** 74
  Michael Jordan-**P,** 139
  Munchkins-**DD,** 40
  Pancake Kids-**IHOP,** 49
  Potato Head Kids-**M, W,** 79,
    110
  Saurus Sports Ball-**W,** 111
  Sports Balls-**M,** 81
  Wild Games-**W,** 114
  Write and Sniff-**W,** 114

Basketball
  Airtoads-**S,** 92
  Brown Bag Juniors-**S,** 93
  Burger King All Stars-**BK,** 19
  Castleburger Dudes-**WC,** 115
  Chuck E Cheese-**SP,** 91
  Franksters-N, 86
  Funny Fry Friends-**M,** 63
  Good Sports-**W,** 108
  Michael Jordan-**P,** 139
  Mini Sports Games-**BK,** 26
  Saurus Sports Ball-**W,** 111
  Sports Balls-**M,** 81
  Wild Games-**W,** 44

Bears
  A&W Bear-**P,** 131
  Animal Squirters-**S,** 92
  Amazing Wildlife-**P,** 130

Babar-**A**, 11
Berenstain Bears-**M**, 59, 65
Cabbage Patch-**M**, 60
Coca Cola Bear-**P**, 134
Crayola Bears-**P**, 134
Dairy Queen Bear-**DQ**, **P**, 32, 34, 134
Disneyland 40th-**M**, 62
Furskins-**P**, 135
Garfield-**M**, 64
Glass Hangers-**S**, **W**, 94, 107
Goodstuff Gang-**W**, 108
Happy Birthday-**M**, 65
Jungle Book-**M**, 67
Kissyfur-**M**, 67
Lisa Frank-**WM**, 108
Muppet Workshop-**M**, 77
Muppets (Fozzie)-**CJ**, **F**, **H**, **M**, **TM**, **P**, 31, 45, 65, 76, 101, 140
Raggedy Ann & Andy-**M**, 80
Rescue Rangers-**M**, 61
Shirt Tales-**P**, 141
Shoney's Bear-**P**, 141
Teddy Ruxpin-**W**, 112
Wild Friends-**M**, 85
Wildlife Rangers-**SW**, 101
World Wildlife Fund-**W**, 144
Yo, Yogi-**M**, 85
Yogi Bear & Friends-**A**, **W**, 12, 15, 16, 114

rds
Aladdin-**BK**, **P**, 17, 131
Animaniacs-**M**, 54
Bambi-**M**, 56
Disney (Donald)-**BK**, **M**, **P**, 26, 29, 75, 139
Ducktales-**M**, 61, 62
Glass Hangers-**S**, **W**, 94, 107
Goodstuff Gang-**W**, 108
Happy Moodie-**W**, 108
Lea Animaux-**F**, 123
Lion King-**BK**, **F**, 25, 123
Looney Tunes-**A**, **F**, 13, 14, 82, 123
McDonald's (Birdie)-**F**, **M**, 69-74, 124-127
Muppet Workshop-**M**, 77
Peanuts-**M**, 78
Pencil Topper-**CFA**, 31
Piggsburg Pigs-**M**, 79
Pocahontas-**BK**, 29
Polar Swirl Penguins-**A**, 15
Rock-A-Doodle-**DQ**, 36
Sea Walkers-**LJS**, 53
Silverhawks-**BK**, 28
Simpsons-**BK**, 28
Super Heroes-**M**, 82

Swan Princess-**H**, 47
Tiny Toons-**M**, 83
Water Blasters-**LJS**, 53
Weird Writers-**W**, 113
Welcome Year of the Rooster-**F**, 128

Boats
Asterix-**F**, 120
Bobby's World-**M**, 60
Burger King Water Mates-**BK**, 21
Disneyland 40th-**M**, 62
Euro-Disney-**F**, 121
Goofy Movie-**BK**, 24
Hook-**M**, 65
Little Mermaid-**M**, 68
Marvel Comics-**H**, 45
McDonald's Feeling Good-**M**, 71
McDonald's Sailors-**M**, 73
McTransports-**F**, 126
Mickey's Toontown Disneyland-**BK**, 26
Push N Go Go Go-**WC**, 116
Sea Watchers-**LJS**, 53
Techno Tows-**W**, 112
Tiny Toons Flip Cars-**M**, 83
Yogi & Friends-**W**, 114

Books-Characters with books
Brown Bag Juniors-**S**, 93
Looney Tunes-**A**, 13

Bowling
Brown Bag Bowlers-**S**, 92
California Raisins-**H**, 42
Flintstones-**F**, 121
Good Sports-**W**, 108
Goof Troup-**BK**, 29

Boxing-Noid-**DP**, 40

Bubblers
Dino-**DQ**, 33
White Castle-**WC**, 118

Buildings/Houses
Capitol Critters-**BK**, 21
Flintstones-**F**, **M**, 62, 121, 122
McAirport-**F**, 124
McTown-F126
McDonald's United Airlines-**M**, 74

Bus
Flintstones Movie-**F**, 122
McTransports-**F**, 126

California Raisins-**H**, 41, 42, 132

Cards-Playing Cards
  Creative Child Cards-**DQ**, 33
  Dennis Deck-**DQ**, 33
  Endangered Animal Games
    -**W**, 106
  Fish Cards-**LJS**, 52
  Go Fish Dinos-**W**, 106

Cars with Characters-1 unit
  Archie Comics-**BK**, 17
  Babar Pullback Racers-**A**, 11
  Babar Vehicles-**A**, 12
  Back to the Future-**M**, 56
  Batman-**M**, 58
  Big Boy Sports-**BB**, 16
  Chuck E Cheese-**SP**, 90
  Dennis the Menace-**DQ**, 33
  Disney 40th-**M**, 62
  Drive Thru Crew-**M**, 61
  Fender Bender-**H, CJ**, 31, 43
  Fish Cars-**LJS**, 52
  Flintstones-**D, F, M**, 38, 62, 122
  Gobots-**W**, 108
  Goofy Movie-**BK**, 24
  Jetsons-**W**, 109
  Looney Tunes-**A**, 13
  Marvel Comics-**H**, 45
  McDonald's Characters-**F, M**,
    71, 72, 73, 124, 126
  McTonight-**M**, 69
  Mickey 's Birthday Land-**M**, 75
  Nicktoons Cruisers-**H**, 45
  Pancake Kids-**IHOP**, 49
  Piggsburg Pigs-**M**, 79
  Purr-Tenders-**BK**, 27
  Spiderman-**M**, 83
  Super Heroes-**H**, 45
  Tiny Toons-**M**, 83
  Tom & Jerry-**DQ, SW**, 36, 99
  Wendy's Food Racers-**W**, 106

Cars with No Character
  Arts-**W**, 105
  Attack Pack-**F, M**, 55, 120
  Big Foot-**M**, 59
  Chuck E Cheese-**SP**, 90
  Custom Cruisers-**S**, 93
  Days of Thunder-**H**, 42
  Happy Birthday-**M**, 65
  Hot Wheels-**M**, 66, 67
  Kentucky Fried Chicken
    -**KFC**, 51
  Matchbox Cars-**BK**, 26
  Mickeys Birthday Land-**M**, 75
  Mighty Minis-**M**, 75
  Pullback Racers-**DQ**, 35
  Record Breakers-**BK**, 27

Road Runner-**H**, 46
Speed Bumpers-**W**, 111
Speed Writers-**W**, 111
Stomper Mini 4x4-**M**, 82
Super Sonic Turbo Racers-**S**,
  95
Techno Tows-**W**, 112
Tonka-**M**, 84
Totally Toy Holiday-Boys-**M**,
  84

Cars with Separate Characters
  Bobby's World-**M**, 60
  Ducktales-**M**, 62
  Flintstone Cruisers-**D**, 38
  Garfield-**M**, 64
  Looney Tunes-**F**, 123
  Muppet Babies-**M**, 76
  Muppet Parade-**CJ**, 31
  Targeteers-**TM**, 102

Cats
  101 Dalmations-**M**, 54
  Aladdin-**BK,P**, 17, 131
  Aliens-**PH**, 87
  Amazing Wildlife-**P**, 130
  Animal Squirters-**S**, 92
  Aristocats-**F**, 120
  Batman-**M**, 58
  Bonkers-**BK**, 18
  Capitol Critters-**BK**, 21
  Disneyland 40th-**M**, 62
  Eek! The Cat-**BK**, 43
  Fun House Faces-**CJ**, 30
  Garfield-**M, PH**, 64, 87
  Halloween McNuggets-**M**, 64
  Holiday Huggables-**P**, 137
  Lion King-**BK, F**, 25, 123
  Lisa Frank-**WM**, 103
  Marsupilami-**PH**, 87
  Nicktoon Cruisers-**H**, 45
  Nightmare Before Xmas-**BK**, 27
  Oliver & Co-**M, P**, 78, 142
  Peanuts-**M**, 78
  Playful Pets-**TM**, 101
  Pick-Nic-**DQ**, 35
  Pinnochio-**P**, 140
  Purr-Tenders-**BK, P**, 27, 141
  Purries & Pound Puppies-**P**,
    140
  Richard Scarry-**CFA, TB**, 32,
    101
  Rock-A-Doodle-**DQ**, 36
  Shirt Tales-**P**, 141
  Swat Kats-**WC**, 117
  Tag-Along-**P**, 143
  Thundercats-**BK**, 29
  Tom & Jerry-**DQ, M, SW**,
    36, 84, 99

Wildlife Rangers-**SW**, 101
World Wildlife Fund-**W**, 144

Christmas
Cabbage Patch-**M**, 60
Christmas Elves-**H**, 46
Christmas Ornaments-**WM**, 102
Cinderella-**P**, 130
Dennis the Menace-**DQ**, 33
Happy Birthday-**M**, 65
Holiday Express-**S**, 94
Holiday Huggables-**P**, 137
Jetsons Puzzle Ornaments-**D**, 39
Little Mermaid-**P**137
Looney Tunes-**A**, 13
Muppet Christmas Carol-**H**, **P**, 45, 140
Nightmare Before Christmas -**BK**, 27
Puzzle Ornaments-**KM**, 51
Rescuers Down Under-**P**, 142
Rodney & Friends-**P**, 142
Rudolph-**P**, 142
Santa Clause-**SW**, 99
Snowballs-**H**, 47
Totally Holiday-**M**, 84, 85
Wacky Wind-Ups-**W**, 113
Walt Disney Mickey's Christmas Carol-**P**, 139

Color Changers/Fluorescent
After Dark-**P**, 133
Captain Planet Rings-**SW**, 97
Casper-**P**, 140
Cosmic Flyers-**KM**, 51
Gargoyles-**BK**, 23
Glo-Ahead-**W**, 107
Glow-in-the-Dark Monsters -**WC**, 116
Marsupilami-**PH**, 87
Snowballs-**H**, 47
Super Sonic Turbo Racer-**S**, 95
Tricky Tints-**W**, 113
UFO-**W**, 113

Costumes
Bone-A-Fide Friends-**CJ**, 30
Dennis the Menace-**DQ**, 33
Super Heroes-**M**, 82
The Swan Princess-**H**, 47

Cowboys & Indians
Barbie-**M**, 57
Funny Fry Friends-**M**, 64
Goofy Movie-**BK**, 24
Looney Tunes-**A**, 13, 14
McNugget Buddies-**M**, 74
Playmobile-**M**, 79

Potato Head Kids-**M, W**, 79, 103
Tall Tales-**SW**, 99
Write & Sniff-**W**, 114

Cycles
Animaniacs-**M**, 54
Aristocats-**F**, 120
Babar-**A**, 12
Barbie-**M**, 58
Batman-**M**, 59
Bobby's World-**M**, 60
Cybercycles-**W**, 104
Ducktales-**M**, 62
Fry Benders-**M**, 63
Garfield-**M**, 64
Los Muppet Bebes-**F**, 123
McCharacters in Sports Vehicles-**F**, 124
McDonald's Connectibles & Linkables-**M**, 71
McDonaldland-**M**, 74
McTonight-**M**, 69
Muppet Babies-**M**, 76
Nicktoons-**H**, 45
Piggsburg Pigs-**M**, 79
Taz Mania Crazies-**F**, 128
Tiny Toons-**M**, 83
Yo, Yogi-**M**, 85

DC Comics-Batman-**M**, 58, 59

Dennis The Menace-**DQ**, 33, 34

Dinos, Dragons, Alligators
Astrosniks-**M**, 55
Bone-A-Fide Friends-**CJ**, 30
Bone Age-**BK**, 18
Christmas Giveaways-**P**, 133
Definitely Dinosaurs-**W**, 105
Dennis the Menace-**DQ**, 33
Dink the Little Dinosaur-**M**, 61
Dino Bubblers-**DQ**, 33
Dino Crawlers-**BK**, 22
Dino Games-**W**, 106
Dino Hops-**S**, 93
Dino Makers-**D**, 37
Dino Puzzles-**CFA, W**, 32, 106
Dino Racers-**D**, 37
Dino Squirters-**S**, 93
Dino Trolls-**DQ**, 34
Dinosaurs in My Pocket-**H**, 43
Dinosaurs-**H, M**, 43, 61
Dragonettes-**F**, 121
Flintstones-**D, H, F, M, P**, 37, 38, 44, 62, 121, 122
Gator Tales-**RR**, 88
Kissyfur-**M**, 67
Land Before Time-**P**, 144
Land of the Lost-**SW**, 98

McDonald's Design-o-Saurs
 -**M**, 71
Mix-Em Up Monsters-**M**, 76
New Food Changeables-**M**, 77
Raging Reptiles-**CJ**-31
Saurus Sports Balls-**W**, 111
Sea Walkers-**LJS**, 53
Teddy Ruxpin-**W**, 112
Terrible Thunderlizards-**H**, 48
Tinosaurs-**M**, 83
Triastic Take Aparts-**CJ, D,
 DQ, WC,** 30, 35, 37, 117

Discs/Flyers
 7-Eleven-7-11, 11
 After Dark-**P**, 133
 Batman-**M**, 58
 Beach Bunnies-**H**, 41
 Burger King All Stars-**BK**, 19
 Camp California-**CJ, H,** 30, 42
 Chuck E Cheese-**SP**, 90, 91
 Colonel-**KFC**, 51
 Cosmic Flyer-**KM**, 51
 Dominos-**DP**, 40
 Honey, I Blew Up the Kid
  -**TB**, 101
 King Burger-**BK**, 24
 McDonald's Flyers-**M**, 72
 Michael Jordan-**M**, 139
 Tricky Tints-**W**, 113
 Wendy's Toys-**W**, 114
 Yogi & Friends-**A**, 15

Disney
 101 Dalmations-**M**, 54
 Aladdin-**BK, F,** 17, 120
 Aladdin Hidden Treasures-**P**,
  131
 Aristocats-**F**, 120
 Bambi-**M**, 56
 Beauty & The Beast-**BK, F, P,**
  17, 121, 132
 Bonkers-**BK**, 18
 Chip 'n' Dale's Rescue
  Rangers-**M**, 61
 Cinderella-**P**, 130
 Dinosaurs-**M**, 61
 Disneyland 40th-**M**, 62
 Ducktales-**M**, 61, 62
 EuroDisney-**F**, 121
 Goof Troup Bowlers-**BK**, 24
 Goofy Movie-**BK**, 24
 Happy Birthday-**M**, 65
 Honey, I Blew Up the Kid-**TB**,
  101
 Jungle Book-**M**, 67
 Little Mermaid-**M, P,** 68, 137
 Little Mermaid Splash
  Collection-**BK**, 26

Lion King-**BK**, 25
Lion King Finger Puppets-**BK**,
 25
Marsupilami Houba-Douba
 -**PH**, 87
Mickey & Friends Epcot
 Center-**M**, 75
Mickey's Birthday Land-**M**, 75
Mickey's Christmas Carol-**P**,
 139
Mickey's Toontown
 Disneyland-**BK**, 26
Oliver & Co-**M, P,** 78, 142
Pinnochio Summer Inflatables
 -**P**, 140
Pocahontas-**BK**, 29
Rescuers Down Under-**M, P,**
 80, 142
Robin Hood Rad Badges-**F**,
 127
Santa Clause-**SW**, 99
Snow White-**M**, 81
Tailspin-**M**, 83
Tall Tales-**SW**, 99
Walt Disney Classics-**P**, 143
Walt Disney World-**BK**, 29

Dogs
 101 Dalmations-**M, P,** 54, 65,
  143
 All Dogs Go To Heaven-**W**, 104
 Animal Squirters-**S**, 92
 Asterix-**F**, 120
 Dogs-**DQ**, 34
 Eek! The Cat-**H**, 43
 Euro Disney-**F**, 121
 Five Lucky Stars-**F**, 121
 Garfield-**M**, 64
 Gliedertiere Floppy Puppets
  -**F**, 122
 Grimmy-**B**, 16
 Happy Birthday-**M**, 65
 Holiday Huggables-**P**, 137
 Jetsons-**D, DQ, W,** 34, 39, 109
 Lisa Frank-**WM**, 103
 Mickey & Friends Epcot
  Center-**M**, 75
 Mickey's Birthday Land-**M**, 75
 Mighty Mouse-**W**, 109
 Muppet Workshop-**M**, 77
 Nicktoons Cruisers-**H**, 45
 Oliver & Co-**M**, 78, 142
 Peanuts-**M**, 78
 Pick-Nic-**DQ**, 35
 Playful Pets-**TM**, 101
 Playmobile-**M**, 79
 Pocahontas-**BK**, 29
 Pound Puppies-**P**, 140
 Puppy in My Pocket-**DQ**,

WC, 35, 116
Purr-Tenders-**BK, P,** 27, 141
Purries & Pound Puppies-**P,** 140
Richard Scarry-**CFA,** 31
Rock-A-Doodle-**DQ,** 36
Scooby Doo-**A,** 15
Showbiz Pizza-**SP,** 91
Smurfs on Skateboards-**H,** 46
Tom & Jerry-**M,** 84
Walt Disney Classics-**P,** 143
Where's Waldo-**H,** 48
White Castle Meal Friends
  -**WC,** 117, 118
Yogi-**M, W,** 85, 114

Elephants
  African Animals-**CFA,** 31
  Amazing Wildlife-**P,** 130
  Babar-**A,** 11, 12
  Disneyland 40th-**M,** 62
  Endangered Animal Games
    -**W,** 106
  Flintstones-**D,** 37, 38
  Glass Hangers-**S, W,** 94, 107
  Gliedertiere-**F,** 122
  Jungle Book-**M,** 67
  Les Animaux-**F,** 123
  McDonald's Circus Parade
    -**M,** 70
  Walt Disney Classics-**P,** 143
  Wild Friends-**M,** 85

Engines/Trains
  Back To The Future-**M,** 56
  Circus Train-**DQ,** 33
  Disneyland 40th-**M,** 62
  Euro Disney-**F,** 121
  Holiday Express-**S,** 94
  Little Engineers-**M,** 72
  Looney Tunes-**F,** 123
  McDonaldland Junction-**M,** 74
  McTransports-**F,** 126
  Mickey's Birthdayland-**M,** 75
  Peanuts-**F,** 127
  Tootsie Roll Express-**WC,** 117

Fairy Tales
  Cinderella-**P,** 130
  Beauty and the Beast-**BK, P,**
    17, 132
  Snow White-**M,** 81
  Swan Princess-**H,** 47

Farms/Farmers
  Chick-Fil-A Pencil Topper
    -**CFA,** 31
  Pancake Kids-**IHOP,** 49
  Peanuts-**M,** 78
  Playmobile-**M,** 79

Fire Engines/Firemen
  Dennis the Menace-**DQ,** 33
  Euro Disney-**F,** 121
  Looney Tunes Fun Figures
    -**A,** 13
  McDonald's Cracy Vehicles
    -**M,** 71
  McNugget Buddies-**M,** 74
  McTown-**F,** 126
  Peanuts-**F,** 127
  Potato Head Kids-**W,** 110
  Write & Sniff-**W,** 114

Finger Puppets/Pencil Toppers
  Alf-**W,** 104
  Babar Tourists-**A,** 11
  Beetlejuice-**BK,** 18
  Capitol Critters-**BK,** 21
  Chick-Fil-A-**CFA,** 31
  Coneheads-**SW,** 97
  Chuck E Cheese-**SP,** 90
  Ghostbusters-**M,** 64
  Glo-Ahead-**W,** 107
  Glo Friends-**W,** 107
  Jack-in-the-Box-Finger
    Puppets-**JB,** 50
  King Burger-**BK,** 24
  Lion King Finger Puppets-**BK,**
    25
  Little Caesar-**LC,** 52
  Looney Tunes Pencil Toppers
    -**A,** 14
  Muppet Christmas Carol-**H,** 45
  New Food Changeables-**M,** 77
  Oliver & Co-**M,** 78
  Popeye Pencil Toppers-**PFC,**
    87
  Richard Scarry-**TB,** 101
  Silverhawks-**BK,** 28
  Simpsons-**BK,** 28
  Super Mario Brothers-**M,** 82
  Treasure Trolls-**CJ, H, LJS,**
    RR, S, 48, 53, 89, 96, 103

Fish/Sea Life
  Asterix-**F,** 120
  Fish Cards-**LJS,** 52
  Go Fish Cars-**LJS,** 52
  Goofy Movie-**BK,** 24
  Little Mermaid-**BK, M, P,**
    26, 68, 137
  Lisa Frank-**WM,** 103
  McRockin Fast Food-**F,** 125
  Sea World of Ohio-**M,** 80
  Sea Walkers-**LJS,** 53
  Sea Watchers-**LJS,** 53
  Water Blasters-**LJS,** 53

151

Flying/Airplanes
  Aladdin-**BK, F,** 17, 102, 130
  Animaniacs-**M,** 54
  Astrosnik-**M,** 55
  Attack Pack-**F, M,** 55, 120
  Babar Vehicles-**A,** 12
  Back to the Future-**M,** 56
  Blimp-**LC,** 52
  Bobby's World-**M,** 60
  Captain Planet Flip Cars-**BK,** 22
  Chip 'n' Dale's Rescue Rangers-**M,** 61
  Ducktales-**M,** 62
  Fun Flyers-**RR,** 88
  Go, Go Gadget-**BK,** 23
  Gobots-**W,** 108
  Jetson's-**DQ, D, W,** 34, 39, 109
  Looney Tunes-**A, F,** 13, 123
  McDonald's-**F, M,** 69, 70, 71, 72, 74, 124, 126
  McTonight-**M,** 69
  Mighty Mouse-**W,** 109
  Muppet Babies-**M,** 76
  Nicktoons Cruisers-**H,** 45
  Peanuts-**F,** 127
  Pilot Taz-**A,** 13
  Push n Go Go Go-**WC,** 116
  Space Shuttle-**DQ,** 36
  Spacebase Racers-**BK,** 28
  Spiderman-**M,** 83
  Super Mario-**M,** 82
  Super Sky Carrier-**W,** 111, 112
  Tailspin-**M,** 83
  Young Astronauts-**M,** 85

Food
  Arts-**W,** 105
  Astrosniks-**M,** 55
  Bag-A-Wag-**S,** 92
  Basic 4-**M,** 58
  Burger King It's Magic-**BK,** 19
  Burger King Kid Transporters -**BK,** 20
  Castleburger Dudes-**WC,** 115, 118, 119
  Chuck E Cheese-**SP,** 91
  Dairy Queen Spinners-**DQ,** 34
  Dennis the Menace-**DQ,** 34
  Dino Hops-**S,** 93
  Drive-Thru Crew-**M,** 61
  Fast Food Miniatures-**BK,** 22
  Fast Food Squirters-**H, S,** 44, 95
  Flying Food-**S,** 94
  Food Racers-**W,** 106
  Fraggle Rock-**M,** 63
  Franksters-**N,** 86
  Fry Benders-**M,** 63
  Fun Bunch-**DQ,** 34
  Fun Food-**BK,** 22
  Fun House Faces-**CJ,** 30
  Fun with Food-**M,** 63
  Good Goblin-**BK,** 23
  Halloween McNuggets-**M,** 64
  Halloween Pez-**WC,** 116
  Happy Birthday-**M,** 65
  Jack-in-the-Box Bendable Buddies-**JB,** 50
  Jack-in-the-Box Finger Puppets-**JB,** 50
  Lickety Splits-**BK,** 25
  Little Caesar-**LC, P,** 52, 137
  McDonald's Circus Parade-**M,** 70
  McMeal-**F,** 125
  McRockin' Fast Food-**F,** 125
  Mr Big Bite-7-11, 11
  Mr Kiasu-**F,** 127
  Munchkins-**DD,** 40
  New Food Changeables-**M,** 77, 78
  Nightmare Before Xmas-**BK,** 27
  Olympic McNuggets-**F,** 127
  Oscar Mayer-7-11, 11
  Pancake Kids-**IHOP,** 49
  Pancake Kids Cruisers-**IHOP,** 49
  Piggsburg Pigs-**M,** 79
  Pizza Hut-**PH,** 87
  Play Yard-**BB,** 16
  Pocahontas-**BK,** 29
  Potato Head Kids-**M, W,** 79, 103
  Purr-Tenders-**BK,** 27
  Targeteers-**TM,** 102
  Tiny Toons Flip Cars-**M,** 83
  Too Cool for School-**W,** 112
  Wacky Wind-Ups-**W,** 113

Football
  Burger King All Stars-**BK,** 19
  Castleburger Dudes Sports Balls-**WC,** 115
  Chuck E Cheese-**SP,** 91
  Discovery Zone-**DZ,** 40
  Franksters-**N,** 86
  Michael Jordan-**P,** 139
  Mini Sports Games-**BK,** 26
  Good Sports-**W,** 108
  Saurus Sports Ball-**W,** 111
  Smurfs-**H,** 46
  Sports Balls **M,** 81
  Wendys Football-**W,** 114

Games
  Burger King It's Magic-**BK,** 19

152

Burger King Top Kids-**BK,** 21
Dino Games-**W,** 106
Endangered Animal Games
 -**W,** 106
Glo-Ahead-**W,** 107
Good Sports-**W,** 108
Jetsons Puzzle Ornaments-**D,** 39
Magic School Bus-**M,** 69
McDonald's Water Games
 -**M,** 73
Mini Sports Games-**BK,** 26
Puzzle Ornaments-**KM**51
Totally Toy Holiday-**M,** 84, 85
Wild Games-**W,** 114

Garfield-**M, PH,** 64, 87

Gladiators-**F,** 122

Gliders
 Flintstones-**D,** 38
 Good Sports-**W,** 108
 Yogi & Friends-**W,** 114

Golf-Good Sports-W108

"Hair"
 Barbie-**F, M,** 58, 121
 Burger King Glow-in-the-
  Dark Trolls-**BK,** 19
 Dino Trolls-**DQ,** 34
 Targeteers-**TM,** 102
 Trolls-**H, LJS, RR, S,
  WM,** 48, 53, 89, 96, 103

Halloween
 Beetlejuice-BK,18
 Burger King Pranks-**BK,** 20
 Casper-**P,** 140
 Fun House Faces-**CJ,** 30
 Gargoyles-**BK,** 23
 Ghostbusters-**H, M,** 44, 64
 Glo Ahead-**W,** 107
 Glow-in-the-Dark Monsters
  -**WC,** 116
 Good Gobblin-**BK,** 23
 Gravedale High-**M,** 64
 Halloween McNugget Buddies
  -**M,** 64
 Halloween Surprises-**P,** 137
 Nightmare Before Christmas
  -**BK,** 27
 Pez-**WC,** 116
 Potato Head Kids-**W,** 110

Hand Puppets
 Alf-P
 Beauty & the Beast-**P,** 132
 Casper-**P,** 135

Eureeka's Castle-**P,** 135
Land Before Time-**P,** 138

Hanna-Barbera
 Crazy Cruisers-Yogi-**A,** 12
 Fender Bender-**CJ, H,** 31, 43
 Flintstones-**F,** 121
 Flintstone's Dino Makers-**D,** 37
 Flintstone's Dino Racers-**D,** 37
 Flintstone's First 30 Years-**H,** 44
 Flintstone's Fun Squirters-**D,** 37
 Flintstone's Glacier Gliders-**D,** 38
 Flintstone's Kids-**M,** 62
 Flintstone's Mini-Plush-**P,** 130
 Flintstone's Movie-**F, M,** 62,122
 Flintstone's Rock N Rollers
  -**D,** 38
 Flintstone's Stone Age Cruisers
  -**D,** 38
 Flintstone's Vehicles-**D,** 38
 Jetson's-**DQ,** 34
 Jetson's Movie-**W,** 109
 Jetson's Planets-**D,** 39
 Jetson's Puzzle Ornaments-**D,** 39
 Jetson's Space Vehicles-**W,** 109
 Jetson's Spacecards-**D,** 39
 Jetson's Stencil-**D,** 37
 Pound Puppies-**P,** 140
 Scooby Doo Silly Putty-**A,** 15
 Shirt Tales-**P,** 135
 Smurfs-**H,** 46
 Smurfs on Skateboards-**H,** 46
 Snorks-**RR,** 89
 Swat Kats-**WC,** 117
 Tom & Jerry-**DQ, M,** SW ,
  36, 84, 99
 Yo, Yogi-**F, M,** 85
 Yogi Bear & Friends Gliders
  -**W,** 114
 Yogi Bear & Friends Mini
  Discs-**A,** 15
 Yogi Bear & Friends Squirters
  -**A,**16

Hats-separate
 Funny Fry Friends-**M,** 63
 Gator Tales-**RR,** 88
 Playmobile-**M,** 79
 Potato Head Kids-**M, W,** 79, 103

Henson
 Fraggle Rock-**M,** 63
 Happy Birthday-**M,** 65
 Los Muppet Bebes-**F,** 123
 Muppets Parade of Stars-**CJ,** 31
 Muppets Christmas Carol-**H,** 45
 Muppet Twisters-**TM,** 101
 Muppet Babies 87 & 90-**M,** 76
 Muppet Babies Christmas

153

Carol-**P,** 140
Muppet Workshop-**M,** 77

Hiking
  Babar Stampers-**A,** 12
  Bag A Wag-**S,** 92
  Barbie-**M,** 58
  Funny Fry Friends-**M,** 63
  Simpsons-**BK,** 28

Hockey
  Burger King All Stars-**BK,** 19
  Franksters-**N,** 86
  Good Sports-**W,** 108

Horses/Rocking Horses
  Goofy Movie-**BK,** 24
  Happy Birthday-**M,** 45
  McDonald's Circus Parade
    -**M,** 70
  Muppet Babies-**M,** 76
  Nicktoon Cruisers-**H,** 45
  Playmobile-**M,** 79
  Snow White-**M,** 81
  Tall Tales-**SW,** 99
  Tinosaurs-**M,** 83
  White Castle Meal Family
    -**WC,** 117, 118

Humans
  101 Dalmations-**M,** 54
  Adventures of the Super Sonic
    Kids-**S,** 92
  All Dogs Go To Heaven-**W,**
    104
  Aristocats-**F,** 120
  Bag A Wag-**S,** 92
  Barbie-**F, M,** 57, 58, 121
  Beetlejuice-**BK,** 18
  Big Boy-**BB,** 16
  Bonkers-**BK,** 18
  Burger King Kids-**BK,** 18, 19,
    20, 21
  Captain Planet-**BK,** 22
  Castle Meal Friends-**WC,** 118
  Checkers-**C,** 31
  Fat Albert-**WC,** 115
  GI Joe-**WM,** 103
  Go, Go Gadget-**BK,** 23
  Goodstuff Gang-**W,** 108
  Hugga Bunch-**P,** 136
  Inspector Gadget-**SW,** 98
  Jack-in-the-Box People-**JB,** 50
  Monkey Trouble-**SW,** 99
  Nicktoons-**H,** 45
  Pocahontas-**BK,** 29
  Scooby Doo-**A,** 15
  Skateboard Gang Kids-**RR,** 89
  Spiderman-**M,** 83

Targeteers-**TM,** 102
Teddy Ruxpin-**W,** 112
Water Blasters-**LJS,** 53
Where's Waldo-**H,** 48
White Castle Meal Friends
  -**WC,** 118
X-Men-**H, RR,** 49, 88
Yogi & Friends-**A, W,** 15, 114

Jet Ski
  Burger King Water Mates
    -**BK,** 21
  Ducktales-**M,** 62
  Los Muppet Bebes-**F,** 123
  McCharacters in Sports
    Vehicles-**F,** 124
  McTonight-**M,** 69
  Yo, Yogi-**M,** 85

Jewelry/Wearables
  Barnyard Commando Cuffs
    -**BK,** 17
  Burger King Pranks-**BK,** 17
  Captain Planet-**SW, WC,** 97,
    115
  Chuck E Cheese-**SP,** 90
  Congo the Movie Watches
    -**TB,** 100
  Ducktales-**M,** 61
  Little Caesar's Ring-**LC,** 52
  *Little Rascals Watches-**LJS**
    -no photo
  M Squad-**M,** 68
  McDonald's Olympic Badges
    -**M,** 73
  Nightmare Before Christmas
    Watches-**BK,** 27
  Polly Pocket-**M,** 79
  Stik Mitts-**WC,** 116

Marbles
  Brown Bag Juniors-**S,** 93

Marvel Comics
  Hulk-**H**-45
  Mr America-**H,** 45
  She Hulk-**H,** 45
  Spiderman-**H, M,** 45, 83
  X-Men-**H, RR,** 49, 88

Movies
  101 Dalmations-**M,** 54
  Aladdin-**BK, F,** 17, 120
  All Dogs go to Heaven-**W,** 104
  Aristocats-**F,** 120
  Back to the Future-**M,** 56
  Bambi-**M,** 56
  Batman-**M,** 58
  Beauty & the Beast-**BK, PH,**

17, 132
Beetlejuice-**BK**, 18
Casper-**PH**, 140
Cinderella-**P**, 130
Coneheads-**SW**, 97
Congo-**TB**, 100
  Days of Thunder-**H**, 42
Ducktales-**M**, 61
Flintstones-**M, F**, 62, 121
Ghostbusters-**H, M**, 44, 64
Goofy-**BK**, 24
Honey, I Blew Up the Kid
  -**TB**, 100
Jetsons-**W**, 109
Jungle Book-**M**, 67
Land Before Time-**P**, 144
Land of the Lost-**SW**, 98
Little Mermaid-**M, P**, 68, 137
Lion King-**BK, F**, 25, 123
Mickey's Xmas Carol-**P**, 139
Monkey Trouble-**SW**, 99
Muppets Xmas Carol-**H, P**,
  45, 140
Nightmare Before Xmas-**BK**, 27
Pinocchio-**P**, 140
Pocahontas-**BK**, 29
Rock A Doodle-**DQ**, 36
Santa Clause-**SW**, 99
Snow White-**M**, 81
Swan Princess-**H**, 47
Tall Tales-**SW**, 99
Teenage Mutant Ninja Turtles
  -**BK**, 28, 29

Musicians
Alf-**P**, 138
Alvin & The Chipmunks-**M**, 54
California Raisins-**H**, 41, 42,
  132
Chuck E Cheese-**SP**, 91, 134
Dinosaurs-**M**, 61
Flintstones Rock & Rollers-**D**,
  38
Happy Birthday-**M**, 65
McBand-**F**, 124
McDonald's Circus Parade-
  M, 70
McNugget Buddies-**M**, 74
McTonight-**M**, 68
Muppet Workshop-**M**, 77
Pancake Kids-**IHOP**, 49
Simpsons-**BK**, 28
Tiny Toons-**M**, 83
Tom & Jerry Band-**M**, 84

Nestles Rabbit-**WC**, 116

Noids-**DP**, 40, 140

Nurses
  Potato Head Kids-**W**, 103
  Smurfs-**H**, 46
  Snorkes-**RR**, 89

Pens
  Arts-**W**, 105
  Bendy Pens-**WC**, 117
  Doodletops-**SW**, 97
  Frosty Pens-**W**, 105
  Pickle Pen-**W**, 112
  Rocket Writers-**W**, 110
  Speed Writeres-**W**, 111
  Weird Writers-**W**, 113
  Write & Sniff-**W**, 114

Pez-Halloween Pez-WC,116

Pirates
  Disneyland 40th-**M**, 62
  Funny Fry Friends-**M**, 63
  Hamburgular-**M**, 70-74
  Hook-**M**, 65
  McDonald's Moveables-**M**, 72
  Monkey Trouble (actually he's
    a Gypsy)-**SW**, 99
  Potato Head Kids-**W**, 103
  Sea Walkers-**LJS**, 53
  Sea Watchers-**LJS**, 53
  Water Blasters-**LJS**, 53

*POGS-no photo of any pog
  *Apollo 13-H
  *Astronauts-LJS
  *Busch Gardens-TB
  *Mighty Morphin Power
    Rangers-M
  *Sea World-TB
  *X-Men-TM
  *Z-Bots-BK

Policemen/Police Cars
  Bonkers-**BK**, 18
  McNugget Buddies-**M**, 74
  Potato Head Kids-**W**, 110
  Richard Scarry-**CFA**, 32

Puzzles
  African Animals-**CFA**, 31, 123
  Dino Games-**W**, 106
  Dino Puzzles-**CFA**, 32
  Endangered Animal Games
    -**W**, 106
  Farm Animals-**CFA**, 32
  Jetsons Ornament Puzzles-**D**,
    39
  K-Mart Puzzle Ornaments
    -**KM**, 51

Robots
  Astrosniks-**M**, 55
  Cy*Treds/Runaway Robots
    -**SW, M**, 80, 97
  Cybercycles-**W**, 104
  Gobots-**W**, 108
  Kid's Pick-Nic-**DQ**, 35
  McMoon Buggies-**F**, 125
  New Food Changeables-**M**, 77
  Number Transformers-**DQ**, 35
  Rosie-Jetsons-**D, DQ**, 34, 39
  Weird Writers-**W**, 113
  Z-Bots-**BK**, 29

Royalty
  Aladdin-**BK, F, P**, 17, 120, 131
  Alf-**W**, 104
  All Dogs Go To Heaven-**W**, 104
  Disneyland 40th-**M**, 62
  Eureeka's Castle-**H, P**, 43, 135
  Jungle Book-**M**, 67
  King Burger-**BK, P**, 24, 129
  Lion King-**BK, F**, 25, 123
  Little Caesar-**LC, P**, 52, 137
  Pocahontas-**BK**, 29
  Potato Head Kids-**W**, 110
  Robin Hood Rad Badges-**F**, 127
  Snow White-**M**, 81
  Swan Princess-**H**, 47
  White Castle Meal Family
    -**WC**, 118

Segmented Bodies
  Dinosaurs-**H**, 43
  Flintstones Dino Makers-**D**, 37
  Funny Fry Friends-**M**, 63
  Mix Em Up Monsters-**M**, 76
  Triastic Take Aparts-**CJ, D, DQ, WC**, 30, 35, 37, 117

Skateboards/Skooters
  Animaniacs-**M**, 54
  Back to the Future-**M**, 56
  Beach Bunnies-**H**, 111
  Berenstain Bears-**M**, 59
  California Raisins-**H**, 42
  Franksters-**N**, 86
  Fry Benders-**M**, 63
  Garfield-**M**, 64
  Lisa Frank-**WM**, 103
  Looney Tunes-**F**, 123
  McCharacters Sports Vehicles
    -**F**, 124
  McTonight-**M**, 69
  Munchkins-**DD**, 40
  Muppet Babies-**M**, 76
  Nicktoons Cruisers-**H**, 45
  Penguins-**A**, 15

Sidewalk Surfers-**S**, 95
Skateboard Gang-**RR**, 89
Smurfs-**H**, 46
Speed Bunnies-**H**, 47
Targeteers-**TM**, 102
Tom & Jerry-**SW**, 99
Yogi-**M, W**, 85, 114

Skating
  Astrosniks-**M**, 55
  Bag A Wag-**S**, 92
  Barbie-**M**, 57
  Basic 4-**M**, 58
  Beach Bunnies-**H**, 41
  Big Boy Sports Figures-**BB**, 16
  Bobby's World-**M**, 60
  Burger King Action Figures
    -**BK**, 18
  Cabbage Patch-**M**, 60
  California Raisins-**H**, 42
  Ducktales-**M**, 62
  Fat Albert-**WC**, 115
  Fry Bender-**M**, 63
  Franksters-**N**, 86
  Flintstone Gliders-**D**, 38
  Funny Fry Friends-**M**, 63
  Garfield-**M**, 64
  Gator Tales-**RR**, 88
  McWinter Sports-**F**, 127
  Muppet Babies-**M**, 76
  Smurf-**H**, 46
  Speed Bunnies-**H**, 47
  Targeteers-TM , 102

Skiing
  Astrosniks-**M**, 55
  Brown Bag Sports-**F**, 93
  Gator Tales-**RR**, 88
  Goofy Movie-**BK**, 24
  Mc Winter Sports-**F**, 127
  Yogi & Friends-**W**, 114

Sleds
  Astrosniks-**M**, 55
  Brown Bag Sports-**S**, 93
  Fat Albert-**WC**, 115
  Flintstones-**D**, 38
  McWinter Sports-**F**, 127
  Yogi & Friends-**A, W**, 12, 114

Smurfs-**H**, 46

Snoopy-**F, M**, 65, 127

Snorks-**RR**, 89

Snow Domes
  Playful Pets-**TM**, 101

Snow Shoes
  Gator Tales-**RR**, 88

Soccer
  Burger King All Stars-**BK**, 19
  Castleburger Dudes Sports
    Balls-**WC**, 115
  Hurricanes-**SW**, 98
  McSports-**F**, 126
  Michael Jordan-**P**, 139
  Mini Sports Games-**BK**, 26
  Monkey Trouble-**SW**, 99
  Saurus Sports Ball-**W**, 111
  Snorkes-**RR**, 89
  Sports Balls-**M**, 81

Spinners
  Camp California-**CJ**, **H**, 30, 42
  Dairy Queen-**DQ**, 34
  Denny's-**D**, 39
  Discovery Zone-**DZ**, 40
  Flying Food-**S**, 94
  Little Caesar-**LC**, 52
  Stunt Grip Geckos-**S**, **WC**,
    96, 117

Squirters
  Animal Squirters-**S**, 92
  Babar Squirters-**A**, 12
  Bobby's World-**M**, 60
  Camp California-**CJ**, **H**, 30, 42
  Dinosaurs-**M**, **S**, 61, 93
  Eek! The Cat-**H**, 43
  Flintstones-**D**, 37
  Fast Food Squirters-**H**, **S**,
    WC, 44, 95, 118
  Goofy Movie-**BK**, 24
  Hook-**M**, 65
  Inspector Gadget-**SW**, 98
  Kid Squirters-**S**, 95
  Leaky Tiki Totems-**KM**, 51
  Little Caesars-**LC**, 52
  Little Mermaid-**BK**, **M**, 26, 68
  McDonald's Water Games
    -**M**, 73
  Micro Super Squirters-**H**, 45
  Shelcore Summer Squirters
    -**WM**, 104
  Snowballs-**H**, 47
  Tom & Jerry-**DQ**, **SW**, 36, 98
  Water Blasters-**LJS**, 53

Stampers
  Babar-**A**, 12
  Eureeka's Castle-**H**, 43
  Inspector Gadget-**SW**, 98
  Rocky & Bullwinkle-**TB**, 101
  Tom & Jerry-**DQ**, 36

Straw Sliders
  Nestle's Rabbit-**WC**, 116
  Once Upon a Forrest-**LJS**, 52
  Thundercats-**BK**, 29
  Where's Waldo-**H**, 48

Suction Cups
  Airtoads-**S**, 92
  Glow Ahead-**W**, 107
  Good Sports-**W**, 108
  Little Mermaid-**M**, 68
  Mighty Mouse-**W**, 109
  Robin Hood Rad Badges-
    F, 127
  Teenage Mutant Ninja
    Turtles-**BK**, 29

Super Heroes
  Aquaman-**BK**, 28
  Captain Planet-**BK**, **SW**, **WC**,
    22, 97, 115
  Gargoyles-**BK**, 23
  Inspector Gadget-**BK**, **SW**,
    23, 98
  Looney Tunes-**M**, 82
  Marvel Comics-**H**, 45
  Mighty Mouse-**W**, 51
  Silverhawk-**BK**, 28
  Sonic the Hedgehog-**F**, **M**,
    81, 128
  Spiderman-**M**, 83
  Stone Protectors-**LJS**, 53
  Super Marlo-**M**, 82
  Super Powers-**BK**, 28
  Teenage Mutant Ninja
    Turtles-**BK**, 28, 29
  Terrible Thunderlizards-**H**, 48
  Thundercats-**H**, 29
  X-Men-**H**, **RR**, 49, 88

Surfboards
  Big Boy Sports Figures-**BB**, 16
  Brown Bag Sports-**S**, 93
  California Raisins-**H**, 42
  Camp California-**CJ**, **H**, 30, 42
  Franksters-**N**, 86
  Go, Go Gadget-**BK**, 23
  Lisa Frank-**WM**, 103
  Smurfs-**H**, 46
  Speed Bunnies-**H**, 47
  Weird Writers-**W**, 113
  Yogi & Friends-**W**, 114

Swimming/Beach
  Alf-**P**, 138
  Babar-**A**, 12
  Barbie-**M**, 57
  Beach Bunnies-**H**, 41
  Bobby's World-**M**, 60

Brown Bag Sports-**S,** 93
Frog-**LC,** 52
Fry Benders-**M,** 63
Go, Go Gadget-**BK,** 23
Hook-M,65
Little Mermaid-**BK, M,** 26, 65, 68
McDonald's Feeling Good -**M,** 71
McNugget Buddies-**M,** 74
Munchkins-**DD,** 40
Polar Swirl Penguins-**A,** 107
Smurfs-**H,** 46
Snorkes-**RR,** 89
Super Powers-**BK,** 28
Yogi & Friends-**W,** 114

Tang Mouths-**H,** 47

Teenage Mutant Ninja Turtles -**BK,** 28, 29

Tom & Jerry-**DQ, M, SW,** 36, 84, 99

Trolls
  Burger King Glow-in-the -Dark Trolls-**BK,** 19
  Dino Trolls-**DQ,** 34
  Treasure Trolls-**H, LJS, RR, S,** 48, 89, 96, 103
  Trolls-**WM,** 103

Two Sided Flippers
  Beetlejuice-**BK,** 18
  Captain Planet-**BK,** 22
  Glo-Ahead-**W,** 107
  Purr-Tenders-**BK,** 27
  Tiny Toons-**M,** 83

Wagons
  Berenstain Bears-**M,** 59
  Bobby's World-**M,** 60
  Fender Bender 500-**CJ, H,** 31, 43
  McDonald's Connectibles & Linkables-**M,** 71
  Muppet Babies-**M,** 76
  Radio Flyer-**DQ,** 35

Walkers
  Sea Walkers-**LJS,** 53
  Swan Princess-**H,** 47

Warner Brothers
  Animaniacs-**M,** 54
  Cartoon Parade-**L,** 51
  Happy Birthday-**M,** 65
  Looney Tunes-**F,** 123
  Looney Tunes Car-Toons-**A,** 13
  Looney Tunes Fun Figures -**A,** 13
  Looney Tunes Holiday Figurines-**A,** 13
  Looney Tunes on Oval Bases -**A,** 14
  Looney Tunes Pencil Toppers -**A,** 14
  Looney Tunes Quack-Up Cars -**M,** 68
  Looney Tunes Straight Legged Characters-**A,** 14
  Super Heroes-**M,** 82
  Taz Mania Crazies-**F,** 128
  Tiny Toons-**M,** 83
  Tiny Toons Flip Cars-**M,** 83

Wheelbarrows
  Berenstain Bears-**M,** 59
  Peanuts-**M,** 78

Whistles
  Ducktales-**M,** 61
  Fun Bunch-**DQ,** 34
  Fun Food-**BK,** 22
  Kazoo Crew Sailors-**H,** 44
  McDonaldland Band-**M,** 74
  Pan Pipes-**LC,** 52

Wildlife
  African Animals-**CFA,** 31
  Amazing Wildlife-**P,** 130
  Circus Train-**DQ,** 33
  Coca-Cola Polar Bear-**P,** 134
  Congo the Movie Watches -**TB,** 100
  Disneyland 40th-**M,** 62
  Endangered Animal Games -**W,** 106
  Lion King-**BK,** 25, 123
  Mutant Jungle Mix-Ups-**TB,** 100
  Tag Along-**P,** 143
  Wild Friends-**M,** 85
  Wild Games-**W,** 114
  Wildlife Rangers-**SW,** 101
  World Wildlife Fund-**P,** 144

Wind-Ups
  Asterix-**F,** 120
  Castleburger Dudes-**WC,** 119
  Goofy Movie-**BK,** 24
  Hook-**M,** 65
  Jungle Book-**M,** 67
  Little Mermaid-**BK,** 26
  Lion King-**F,** 123
  McBand-**F,** 124
  McRockin Fast Food-**F,**

McSpace-**F**, 126
McSports-**F**, 126
McTransports-**F**, 126
McWinter Sports-**F**, 127
Mickey's Toontown-**BK**, 26
Mighty Mini-**M**, 75
Pocahontas-**BK**, 29
Sonic the Hedgehog-**M**, 81
Taz Mania Crazies-**F**, 128
Techno Tows-**W**, 112
Wacky Wind Ups-**W**, 113

Window Walkers
Adventure Team-**TM**, 101
McDonald's Akrobat-**F**, 124

Winter/Snow
Astrosniks-**M**, 55
Brown Bag Sports-**S**, 93
Cabbage Patch-**M**, 60
Fat Albert-**DQ**,
Flintstone Gliders-**D**, 38
Gator Tales-**RR**, 88
McWinter Sports-**F**, 127
Playful Pets-**TM**, 101
Snowballs-**H**, 47
Yogi-**A**, **W**, 12, 114

MORE FAST FOOD READING FROM...

Welcome to the world of McDonald's® Happy Meal® collectibles. These two books (USA and Worldwide) present a thorough list and complete Price Guide for the thousands of toys and collectibles distributed with Happy Meal® boxes and bags. Together, they are the most authoritative references. Thousands of all-color photographs show the toys, boxes, bags, advertising materials, buttons, pins, and variations given out both in the United States (one book) and in all the other countries around the world (another book).

The authors have established a definitive numbering system to identify each and every item distributed with an alphabetical/numerical listing, and a cross-reference superceding numbering systems in other books.

This set of books gives a time line of McDonald's Corporation history, check-off boxes to help you organize your collection, and the catalog of the items distributed with a Happy Meal® in the USA and worldwide. Read along and enjoy the fun!

Terry and Joyce Losonsky, from Columbia, Maryland, produced the very first collector's guide to Happy Meal® collectibles in 1990 and have built a reputation for their accuracy and completeness in this collectibles field ever since. $24.95

SCHIFFER PUBLISHING

77 Lower Valley Road. Atglen, PA 19310
(610) 593-1777